Praise for *Human*

Much like Grandpa used to, Art ha: story that's dear to him while teachi tive leader. His willingness to let his guard down and share his life with the reader is truly unique and doesn't leave for many a dry eye.

—*Rick DeGolia, Executive Chairman at Intellipark*

I thoroughly enjoyed this book. It is chock-full of inspiring nuggets. Art has a winner here.

—*Julie Lyle, Advisor, Investor DemandJump*

Art is a masterful storyteller who takes you gently by the hand and, with humor and charm, guides you through the common pitfalls of being human, then poignantly shows you how connecting with others is key to living a more abundant life.

—*Tanaquil Arduin, Manager, Netherlands Ministry of the Interior and Kingdom Relations*

In a world seemingly bent on dividing and disconnecting us, how refreshing it is to immerse one's self in the importance of deep, genuine connection. Coombs has done it again—weaving a rich tapestry of personal narrative, historical accounts, and just plain common sense to drive home the importance of human connection and how to create it in our lives, at home, and at work. I will be reading and recommending this book again and again!

—*Robin Jurkowski, Director, Customer Care, Collegis Education*

Mr. Coombs grabbed my attention years ago at a conference in Florida. I knew there was something unique about him when he brought his children into the presentation room. His honesty, sincerity, and desire to include his family in his endeavors reminds me of the type of relationship I can only hope to have with my kids one day. This is a book on leading in life—career leadership included at no additional cost.

—Tom Gene Watkins, Professional Writer

Human Connection will make you smile, laugh, think, and shed a tear or two. Art easily held my attention with his conversational style and heartwarming stories. I adored *Don't Just Manage—LEAD!* However, Art has taken his storytelling to another level with *Human Connection*. I will be giving several copies as a Christmas gift this year. I give this read two huge thumbs-up, five stars, ten out of ten. One of the best books I have ever read.

—David Henderson, AVP, Jacada

Human Connection

How the "L" Do We Do That?

Other Books by Art Combs

Don't Just Manage—Lead!

Human Connection

How the "L" Do We Do That?

Laughing
Learning
Leading
Loving &
Living Large

By Arthur F. Coombs III

Editorial work and production management by Eschler Editing
Cover design by Jennifer Elliott
Interior print design and layout by Ben T. Welch
Published by Scrivener Books

First Edition: September 2017
Printed in the United States of America

10 9 8 7 6 5 4 3 2 1

ISBN 978-0-9986254-2-3 (Paperback)

ACKNOWLEDGMENTS

—————————— ❦ ——————————

IT WOULD BE INAPPROPRIATE not to acknowledge and thank a few of the people who have helped so immensely in writing this book. First, my children. All four have been so supportive with their ideas, love, and permission. My heart is especially tender toward Kai and Mac because they are still at home and watched me spend many evenings in my office slaving away on my laptop when I should have been paying more attention and "connecting" with them. Thanks so much for allowing Dad some alone time to crank this one out.

To my Kathy, you are editor, but more than that you are friend. I cannot thank you enough for your collaborative knack of synching with this dyslexic dude.

To Alice, thanks for stepping in when I needed help. Your contributions were invaluable. You are the consummate professional, and yet it's the laughs we have on silly, meaningless subjects I enjoy most. I am indebted to you.

To Angela and your crew. I love the unruffled, proficient way you go about the business of trying to make me look good. I know that is not easy. My hat is off to you and your team.

WHEN I was twelve years old, I wrote a poem about my father. Years after his passing, it still hangs in my parents' guest room. I cannot count the number of times I have passed by that poem and read the words I wrote over forty years ago in tribute to that great man. While I smile and remember our father-son relationship and how much he meant to me, I have on occasion thought that I should take the time to write a poem for my mother as well.

Mom, this is way overdue. Please forgive me.

I Love You More

You walked me to school,
Five years old that first day—
One nervous, shy boy,
Holding my hand all the way.

You never let go
As we strolled along,

Reassuring my fears,
Keeping me strong.

"You will have fun,"
You said with a smile.
I just held your hand,
Feeling safe all the while.

There came a pause;
Neither one of us spoke.
Then squeeze, squeeze, squeeze,
The silence I broke.

You smiled down at me
And asked, "What does that mean?"
"I love you," I said.
Your smile was serene.

Without saying a word,
You squeezed me four.
"You know what that means?"
You said, "I love you more."

My first day of class,
Not a memory thereof.
Yet vivid are the feelings
Of mother-son and love.

There is nothing else;
The day is a blur.

Still, holding your hand,
The way we were—

That, I remember
Clear as can be.
And saying, "I Love You."
Squeeze one, two, and three.

Fifty years later,
Still squeezing galore.
Squeeze, squeeze, squeeze, squeeze.
You reply, "I love you more."

As a parent, the days and nights can feel so long, and yet when we look back, the years seem so short. Mom, it seems like yesterday you were holding my hand and walking me to school. It seems like yesterday we were pressing our hips into the green leather recliner side by side as you read to me. It seems like yesterday you attended my wrestling matches only to sit in the stands and involuntarily yell, "Hey, he is hurting my boy!"

Thank you for always being there. Thank you for always wanting the best for me and my siblings. Thank you for holding my hand as we walked to school. I love you, Mom, and yet I genuinely believe you do love me more. We do not always see eye-to-eye, but I have never once doubted your reason and cause. You have the purest motives I know of. I love you with all my heart. Squeeze, squeeze, squeeze.

ABOUT TWELVE YEARS AGO, Art and I found ourselves alone in the lavish, opulent office of the CEO of a billion-dollar corporation. The office, located in a high-rise in a major US city, was larger than our entire start-up company's office space. While we waited for the CEO to return (he had excused himself for some pressing matter), we both felt fortunate our small start-up had landed such an appointment. We had a great business concept, the beginnings of a software product, and a small but effective team. In this extraordinary circumstance, we some-how got into a discussion that struck us as so funny we both be-gan laughing uncontrollably—the kind of laughter where your eyes water, your voice sounds like a prepubescent schoolboy, and your body shakes as you try to hold it back. We desperately tried to compose ourselves before the CEO returned lest we to-tally blow this rare opportunity to have an audience with him. But every time we looked at each other, it all started over again.

This was not the first, nor would it be the last, of laughing episodes in our twenty-plus years of working together. This one ended well. We composed ourselves and eventually closed a more-than-million-dollar deal that gave our start-up company a great boost.

I first met Art in the Netherlands in 1996. I was a new expat running customer service for a large software provider in Europe, the Middle East, and Africa regions. Art had been in Holland for a few years already, and though we didn't work for the same company, he reached out and offered to show me the ropes for an American family living in Holland. Among other things, he showed me where to find and buy Cap'n Crunch cereal, maple syrup, turkey, and other items not readily available in Europe at that time. Art had nothing monetary to gain by offering this help, but he did gain a connection and a friend for life. Within two years, he and I would start a business process outsourcing (BPO) organization together, which, within a short period of time, grew to over one thousand employees. With Art's leadership, this company embraced the five *L*'s discussed in this book. Along with hard work and great people, I credit our tremendous success as a company to the application of these principles.

In our current business venture, Art and I regularly get away from the office to have lunch together. While we both left the BPO company over fifteen years ago, it is not uncommon—while we're eating lunch—for one of its former employees to approach us and express how much that job (and Art's leadership) positively influenced their career and life. In fact, most of the early leaders of this BPO have gone on to become very successful leaders in business and other disciplines. One is currently a member of the US Congress. In both public and private relationships, Art has helped countless people launch or improve their careers or simply learn to be more effective in their relationships.

In this book, you'll get a good sense of what it's like knowing and working with Art. You may start to feel, like I do, that you also know his dad, his kids, and his friends—or at least you can relate them to someone you know. Most, if not all, people have experiences from their lives that are worth telling. From this book, you will gain insights about how you can find life lessons within your own experiences and relationships—and then how to better share these with family, friends, and coworkers. You'll learn how to make better connections with these same people and more fully enjoy life's journey with them, especially with people you find more challenging. While this book focuses on connecting, it also teaches about disconnecting with poor behaviors and ineffective ways of thinking. It certainly fits well into the business-leadership genre but could just as easily fit into personal development. Perhaps *Human Connection* illustrates how these are virtually inseparable.

In most respects, Art and I come from opposite backgrounds: he the California Bay Area high school athlete, me the small-town Idaho nerd. We have many divergent views and approaches to politics, religion, and human interactions, yet we have connected on a very personal level throughout the years. As this book so artfully (no pun intended) shows, our personal differences are free of judgment, shaming, or criticism. They are simply differences, ones we have both come to appreciate and embrace.

—*Ronnie Johansen, friend first, business partner second*

Fishing, Fatherhood, and the Other Side of Fifty

SEVERAL YEARS AGO, on a crisp fall Saturday afternoon in Pleasant Grove, Utah, I pulled my fishing poles, tackle box, and several folding camp chairs down from the dusty shelves in the garage and threw them in the back of the truck. I then loaded my three youngest kids (ages twelve, five, and four at the time) and our two golden retrievers into the Dodge, ready to head up into the Rocky Mountains for an afternoon of fishing. Since it can be sunny and eighties in the valley but twenty degrees cooler with the chance of sudden storms in the high country, I made sure we had enough layers to put on and take off depending on the temperature, and we were off.

My two youngest had never been fishing before, and I'd paused for a moment when they'd invited themselves. I am quite certain their interest was being deeply yet discreetly encouraged by their mother, who was most likely envisioning a youngster-free afternoon of soaking in a hot jacuzzi tub with a good book. But their eager smiles and enthusiasm were too much to resist.

You never really know how exciting the fishing will be— sometimes they are jumping and hitting your line like crazy, and other times you are bum-numbingly bored and forced to take in the incredible scenery of mountains and pine-tree-lined lakes. On the way up the mountain, while listening to James Taylor tunes and my kid's chatter, I wondered how long my two youngest would last on this angling outing.

Would I be doing more toddler-tending, or would I actually be fishing? What if one of them slipped into the water? Worse yet, what if they both went in? That water was cold, and I didn't have extra clothes for them. What if they started throwing rocks and disturbed the other fishermen nearby? I mused that this would absolutely happen since I had never seen a child near a body of water who did not have the urge to launch baseball-sized rocks only to delight in the kerplunk sound and size of the splash. Or what if they needed to go potty and the local forest-ranger-maintained facilities were out of commission? What if the fish were still lethargic from the long, warm summer days and it was slow and unexciting? I knew full well how quickly a toddler could get uninterested and then start exploring things they ought not. These questions swirled about in my brain throughout most of the drive.

I typically did not take my dogs fishing, but this time there was a method to my madness. The dogs were there to act, in large part, as nannies to the two younger kids. In our home, my children treated the dogs as family members, and I swear the dogs saw it as their sole purpose to befriend, play with, and protect my children. More than once has a newcomer thought twice about entering our yard, especially if the kids were in the back playing. Once the newcomer was officially sniffed out and past the canine screening, the dogs were true sweethearts. So, inviting the dogs would hopefully provide playmates for the kids should the fishing wane. Meanwhile, my twelve-year-old and I could focus on the tasks at hand—keeping the bait on the hooks, lines in the water, and, hopefully, fish on the stringer.

Before turning off the main road, we stopped at a Sinclair filling station and country store. I topped off the truck with some diesel, and then we all went inside to get a treat and a drink. My kids got candy, beef jerky, some Pop-Tarts, and icies. While I was buying night crawlers, my five-year-old son, Kai, walked up behind me. He stood there a moment or two and then looked at me and said, "Daddy, are those your treats?"

Never one to miss an opportunity to have a little fun, I said, "They sure are." He just stood there with a confused yet trusting look on his face. I then knelt beside him and opened one of the small Styrofoam containers to show him the wiggling night crawlers squirming around. He leaned back in disgust, his brow furrowed and his nose crinkled. I held them a bit closer to him and asked, "Do you wanna try one? That fat one here, I'll bet, is nice and juicy."

Still looking at me, I could see his five-year-old brain churning away and trying to figure out if I were serious or joking. Then his face beamed with the biggest grin ever, and he said, "Daddy, we can always tell when you're joking. Your face makes a funny look."

I chuckled and said, "Yep, Kai, I was just kidding."

But Kai persisted. "If they are not for you, who are they for?"

As I was rounding up his brother and sister and herding them toward the cashier, I said, "Kai, this is what we use for bait. This is what we use to catch the fish."

He looked up at me and said, "Oh, those are the fishes' treats."

Again I chuckled. "Yes, you could say that. These are the fishes' treats."

Even on a fun fishing trip, my boy was looking to me to teach him. As a father, I could have corrected him and said, "This is fish bait" and left it at that. But I wanted to educate, entertain, and connect at the same time. Plus, the fact that he could tell by my facial expression that I was teasing was a clear indication he had seen and connected with that "funny look" before.

After paying for our haul and before leaving the store, I said, "Okay, if you need to use the restroom, now is the time to do it." With that, we all put our bags of goodies on the cashier's counter and went to the back of the store, down a hallway lined with pictures of local fisherman, hunters, and their most recent trophies, and found both the ladies' and gentlemen's restrooms.

As my two boys went to the men's room, I cracked open the ladies'-room door and sheepishly asked, "Is anyone in here?" No reply, so the coast was clear. I had my little Mac (short for Mary Ashely Coombs) go into one of the stalls and told her I would be right on the other side of the semiprivate wall, waiting by the sink. I wiped down the toilet seat, knowing that her little hands would have to prevent her tiny, four-year-old fanny from falling in. I made sure she was settled and then shut the stall door so she could have some privacy.

After about ten seconds, I heard Mac call out, "Daddy, are you there?"

"Yes, baby, Daddy is here."

A few seconds later. "Daddy, are you still there?"

"Yes, honey, Daddy is still here."

"But, Daddy, I cannot see you." I could hear a slight nervousness in her voice.

"Baby girl, you may not see me, but I promise I am here."

"Okay, Daddy, just do not leave me."

"I promise, little girl; your Daddy will never leave you. You may not always see me, but I promise I will always be here for you."

"Okay, Daddy." There was a pause in our conversation. "Daddy?" she said again.

"Yes, Mac?" I replied. Then I heard those words that instantly melt any parent's heart.

"I love you."

There I stood, leaning against a sink in a rather unsanitary ladies' restroom in a country store, wearing old Levi's, a flannel shirt, boots, and a sweat-stained cowboy hat—and my eyes were involuntarily going moist. I instantly thought of my mom and how we'd had a similar conversation about forty-five years earlier while walking to my first day of kindergarten.

I gathered my thoughts and said, "Mackey, want to know what?"

"Yes, Daddy. What?"

"I love you more."

There was a longer than usual pause, then Mac stated, "But, Daddy, I still cannot see you."

I couldn't help but laugh.

The rest of the trip went well. My two youngest played with their four-legged furry sitters, they each caught their very first fish, and my older son and I had a great time catching a few ourselves. But the restroom experience I'd had with my youngest that day was priceless, and I have never forgotten it. I can still hear Mac's small tender four-year-old voice call out, "Daddy, are you there?" And every time that memory crosses my mind, a piece of me melts.

Our children need us to be present. They want to hear us; they want to see us. They need reassurance that we are engaged and present in their lives. It is essential that we are connected with them and that they are connected with us. And while I know there is a critical need in society to be more connected as families, this deep and inherent need for connection extends to friends, workmates, neighbors, and beyond—regardless of whether we consider ourselves introverts or extroverts.

More and more in our precariously shifting world, I see divisiveness, cynicism, disconnection, isolation, loneliness, anxiety, judgment, and despair. People desperately want to connect with others *in person*. They want to laugh, learn, love, live, and be led by leaders and mentors who genuinely care for them. They crave friendship they can trust, lean into, and count on. They want to be accepted for who they are and not shunned for who and what they are not. And the older I get, the more I see the value in true connection and the emptiness of a society created around the falsehoods of maintaining a perfect life online.

Something mysteriously magical happened when I started looking at life from the other side of fifty. Perhaps my white-gray hair gave me some supernatural power I never had before. Maybe I am just mature enough to realize that I honestly do not care what others think anymore. Whatever it is, I have been set free to act and live in a way that makes me whole and cozy in my own skin. I have a boldness and a nonchalant attitude about not impressing others.

This doesn't mean I've become a grumpy old man who gets a daily dose of humor by offending others. It does mean I no longer sugarcoat the truth, nor do I avoid "taboo" issues. I do not need to hoard all my life experiences and wisdom when I can and should be mentoring others. When this magical I-don't-give-a-rat's-ass transformation happens to you, and I hope it happens to you sooner than later, I believe you owe it to this world to share your wisdom, advice, and the sagacious secrets you have learned over the years. Let others learn from your failures and victories. Whether you know it or not, there are some in your circle crying out, just like my daughter did: "Hey, are you there? Please do not leave me."

When you start pushing the senior-citizen threshold, you're immediately put in this position of statesman and wise Yoda-like guidance giver. You are given more liberty to share your thoughts and opinions because you have lived and seen more than most of those around you. I find myself doing and saying bold and crazy things I could never have done or said thirty, twenty, or even ten years ago. But when you share with love, you will be given the respect, deference, and attention granted to those brave enough to stand up and be heard. You will connect with others who need your guidance and, in the process, enrich your life and theirs.

So, for all you senior citizens out there, and, yes, I consider myself among your ranks, don't be shy! Humbly, sincerely, and authentically tell future generations your story. Tell them those things you wish you could have learned thirty years earlier. Grab them by the ears, neck, or elbows. Get their attention and start talking.

Every single person I know has fears, worries, and concerns about the future. Younger generations doubt the world we live in and need our guidance now more than ever. The world we grew up in is vastly different from the one they are growing up in now. Our insights concerning laughing, learning, leading, loving, and living large are more valuable and more needed today than ever before. The masses call out to us, "Hey, are you there? Is anyone there?" In a world full of technology and social media platforms, there's an entire generation (or two) that does not know how to truly connect in person.

We must be bold enough to be present. We must have the integrity to answer the call from both younger generations and our own peers who have drifted away from meaningful connection, and when they indicate they feel alone, like my daughter did at the store, we can say, "Yes, I am here. I will not leave you. You are safe with me."

When the connection is real, and over time you have helped someone expand their heart and horizon, they will say with either their words or through their actions, "Thank you. I love you."

And you can answer back, "I love you more."

Connection: How the "L" Do We do That?

CONNECTING WITH OTHERS is one of the most important things we can do in life. The more effectively we connect, the happier we will be. There are millions and millions of people—teenagers, young adults, middle-agers, and some senior citizens—spread across this planet at this very moment who are extremely connected to others through social media apps but who are desperately lonely and lost. Likewise, there are some who are wonderfully content and fulfilled with only a handful of true, lasting friendships and relationships who don't give a rip about Twitter, Facebook, or Instagram numbers. Our goal in making meaningful connections isn't in quantity but in quality.

So what is human connection, really, and how do we make it meaningful and lasting? As I thought about connection and relationships in my life, I was led down a path of discovering the various ways in which we can become interconnected, as well as the importance of how, when, why, where, and with whom we connect. I broke it down into five sections; Laughing, Learning, Leading, Loving, and Living. I know, I know, I know. Five *L*'s—how convenient. Queue the eye rolling, skepticism, and reluctance to read on. But bear with me, because each one of these areas is mandatory for a well-lived life.

Before we get into the *L*'s, let's spend a little time on connecting and its counterpart, disconnection, and why they are both important. There are many definitions of what it means to connect with others in a positive, healthy way. Let's first define connection, as I see it. Connection is the trust, vitality, and esteem felt between two people when they are understood and respected, and when they are free to share and reveal with no fear of shame, judgment, or ridicule. Connection comes when we are uplifted and renewed by the relationship and when we receive energy, honesty, and life from time spent together. If you do not like my definition, let me slightly adjust Supreme Court Justice Stewart's 1964 famous "I know it when I see it"[1] phrase to make a similar statement (albeit a bit less famous) regarding human-to-human, real connectivity: *I know it when I experience it.* When we connect, we feel it; when we feel it, we know it.

Disconnection, by comparison, is when we've either intentionally shut ourselves off from the rest of the world or when we think we are connecting but the connection is superficial, shallow, or meaningless. This is what we often get in a social-media-crazed society where followers, friends, and "connections" are somehow a measure of your popularity, status, and self-esteem.

Folks, we are here to connect with one another. I mean *genuinely* connect. Human connection is accomplished through empathetic listening, love, softness, acceptance, tolerance, humility, touch, and laughter. When we connect, we instinctually laugh, learn, lead, love, and live with others on a mutually beneficial level. This connection is warm, inclusive, nonjudgmental, and enlightening. The greatest sensation ever is learning you are appreciated by another even though they see your blemishes and stains. A true friend will smile, hold their hand out, and say, "It's okay. With me you are safe, loved, and cared for, blemishes and all." And bam—you feel love and experience connection.

Now, unless you have been living in an isolation chamber, a doomsday bunker, or a hut on the Kerguelen Islands your entire life, you know that eating a healthy diet, getting a good night's sleep, and regular exercise are critical for physical and mental health. It is important to take care of yourself physically to live a long and happy life. (I will let your inner mother beat that drum.) But did you know that your connections and friendships with others are just as important? Studies have shown that being part of a tribe and connected in a social framework (not the same as social media, so please do not confuse this with your follower or friend counts) improves not only mental and emotional health but physical happiness as well. When we are connected with others, the probability of living a long, happy life is radically increased. One study indicated that an absence of real connection does more damage to your health than smoking, obesity, and high blood pressure!

Health specialists are alarmed by the "rampant obesity" crisis we see these days. Yet few seemed to be concerned with the "loneliness and disconnected" crisis, likely because there aren't many scientific studies on the link between health and connection. While we can recognize obesity by simply looking at a person, most lonely people will not admit they are lonely. When you are overweight, it is hard to hide it. You see it, and everyone else does as well. But when you are depressed and lonely, you can walk through this life smiling, pretending, and hiding all those disconnected, isolated feelings from others. All too often we see how truly lonely and frustrated a person is only after it's manifested in some form of destructive behavior. Unfortunately, loneliness, depression, and disconnectedness have a negative stigma that further motivates people to hide or deny their feelings. Obesity, while also associated with negative stigmas, is easy to see; loneliness is easy to miss.

Our moms were right: we should eat our vegetables, get a good night's rest, and enjoy regular physical exercise. But please do not neglect your community of family and friends.

Encourage your children to get off their handheld devices, tablets, gaming consoles, and asses and go play and connect with their friends across the street in a lively game of hide-and-seek, sardines in a can, red rover, or in riding bikes. If you live near a park or community center, get outside and prepare for some serious fun!

As we dive into connection and what it is, I think it is important we also talk about what it isn't. If you agree with my definition above, you'll most likely agree with my basic definition of disconnection; that is, distrust, lifelessness, and contempt felt between two people as they interact with one another. They are not free to share and reveal because there is a sense of fear, shame, judgment, or isolation that spreads out like the Valdez oil spill contaminating the Prince William Sound anytime you are together. There is a sucking of energy, honesty, and life as a result of the relationship. If these feelings of disconnection are not curbed, they will grow into contention, separation, and anger. While one friend will uplift, excite, and renew you when you spend time with them, the other depresses, exhausts, and drains you. Again, you know it when you see it, feel it, and experience it.

You're probably thinking of one or two people right now who are energy suckers in your life. So what do you suppose happens to your psyche (and life as you know it) when an entire nation becomes disconnected? Not that hard to imagine, is it?

Death and Disconnection: The Civil War

Let's take a few moments and chat about the most massively macrounconnected US-centric experience I can think of: the American Civil War. Do not fear—this is not a history book! However, taking a few moments to talk about disconnection is one of the most poignant ways I can think of to plunge into connection itself.

If you paid attention during your junior high US history class, you may remember that approximately 620,000 American soldiers died during this conflict. While war and death of any kind are horrific, massive death on any scale is hard to comprehend. Let's try to put this United States carnage into perspective. If you were to take all American lives lost in World War I, World War II, Vietnam, and Korea, the total of these awful deaths combined would still not be as many as what we lost during the Civil War.

Now, let's take that one step further and look at the largest, bloodiest conflict of the US Civil War—the Battle of Gettysburg, Pennsylvania, where a total of fifty-one thousand men were killed, wounded, or went missing. It was the most violent, bloody, costly battle ever fought in the Western Hemisphere. Tens of thousands of lifeless soldiers lay where they fell. Many were never moved and were buried in shallow graves in the fields of local farmers. And thousands more were left exposed, rotting and decaying in the stifling-hot summer sun. You can probably imagine the sight, but I doubt you can imagine the stench or the soul-sucking feelings of sorrow and confusion for those left behind on the fields of war. The people of Gettysburg had to do something.

It would be a vast understatement to say that all 2,400 citizens of Gettysburg were more than a little overwhelmed by the carnage, smell of death, and emotional trauma of the battle. They were still trying to cope with the immense struggle when President Lincoln, numerous dignitaries, and approximately fifteen thousand others came to Gettysburg to consecrate a cemetery for the Union soldiers who had died there.

If you cannot tell by now, I love history. I am also a raving Abraham Lincoln enthusiast. His "Gettysburg Address" is one of the most divinely crafted, powerfully succinct documents I have ever read. I had the opportunity to visit Gettysburg, Pennsylvania, with one of my best friends and our sons and to walk those consecrated fields. I stood on the field where they say Lincoln stood when he gave the Gettysburg Address, closed my eyes, and tried to soak it in. I tried to turn back time and be one of the thousands in the crowd. In two and a half minutes, Lincoln taught us about the horrors of war and about human dignity, equality, freedom, and national unity. A few months after the horrific battle that represented the pinnacle of disconnection and distrust, Lincoln began to bind up the emotional wounds, soothe souls, and unite a deeply divided country. He was forever focused on the unity of our nation. He was obsessed with our connection with one another. He was fanatically fixated on preserving the Union. And he was a magnificent speaker. But did you know that after his short speech, Lincoln thought he'd bombed?

The featured speaker had rattled on for two hours; Lincoln had spoken for just over two minutes. When he sat down after speaking, he noticed there was an odd silence and a dazed look on most of the faces in the crowd. It appeared the audience was stunned. There was little to no applause. Perhaps he'd caught them off guard with his brevity. Perhaps the contrast to the first speech was too much for them to handle emotionally. Perhaps the crowd had felt the solemn occasion called for a long, drawn-out discourse. Perhaps the attendees were as captivated and awestruck then as we are now at how succinct, powerful, and poignant Lincoln's words were. Whatever the reason, the crowd's reaction, or lack of reaction, caused him to assume his speech—one of the best ever delivered—*wasn't good and wasn't well received.*

Now that, I can truly relate to. Not that I fancy myself as good a speaker as Abe, but I have on a few occasions given a presentation only to have some in the audience look at me in bewilderment and with obviously forced smiles and others with pan-faced, blank stares. Can you see me chuckling? Back to Gettysburg and Lincoln.

We rarely hear about the headlining speaker that day, but it was Edward Everett, an esteemed, famous orator, former secretary of state, and educator. He spoke for two long hours before Lincoln stood and captivated the crowd's attention for just over two minutes. Have you ever read Everett's Gettysburg speech? Probably not. Can it be found in history books anywhere? Maybe if you dig deep, you can find a copy somewhere. Is his oration memorialized or revered by most on this planet? Nope. Not at all.

The day after the speeches were given, Everett wrote Lincoln a letter and said, "I should be glad, if I could flatter myself that

I came as near to the central idea of the occasion, in two hours, as you did in two minutes."

Lincoln's response to Everett: "I am glad to know the speech was not a total failure."[2]

You would think that this book on connection and how we as humans relate to each other would be easier to pull together than the massive combined topics of war, sacrifice, dignity, equality, freedom, and unity Lincoln pulled together. You would think that. But I am no Lincoln. Not even close.

I cannot possibly illustrate how laughing, learning, leading, loving, and living all play a critical role in human-to-human connection in 272 words, as did Lincoln. No way. But I will pour my heart, might, mind, and soul into this work for your benefit. I will write, teach, and demonstrate through the telling of stories (mostly personal) because I believe storytelling is one of the best ways to form a genuine connection with another person. In fact, sharing our stories is an excellent way to allow others into our lives and to be invited into the lives of others. As we share our true selves, we proactively and intentionally create the world around us.

You Create Your Own World

Truth, authenticity, and vulnerability start with you. When you are brave enough to drop your mask and be utterly honest, others are more likely to follow your lead. They will mirror and draw strength from your courage.

I am reminded of a cowboy story an old rancher friend told me once while sitting around a campfire one night.

There was once a lone cowhand working from ranch to ranch, town to town, doing whatever he could to earn buck and board. One day in between jobs, the cowboy rode into a sleepy little town and pointed his sweaty, tired buckskin directly in the direction of the local saloon. Eager to rest his feet, quench his thirst, and get a little information, he walked in and started chatting with the bartender. The old barkeep seemed more than happy to relax for a bit and yak with the young wrangler.

"Hey, old timer," the young fella said. "You look like you have lived here awhile. What sort of folks live in this town?"

The old bartender nonchalantly glanced around the room, pushed his wide-brimmed, sweat-stained hat up with his index finger, looked at the young man, and while squinting his eyes, asked, "Well, young fella, what were the folks like in the town you just came from?"

The cowboy looked at the old man, shook his head in disgust, and said, "Hell, they were a bunch of varmints. All rabble-rousers. They were lazy as the dickens and just sat around and made trouble. They were the most selfish group I ever met; I could not trust a soul. That is why I am here, and between you and me, I am glad they are in my past."

The bartender listened intently and said, "Is that so? I am sorry to hear that. Well, I'm afraid you'll find the same kind in this town as well."

After another drink, the young cowpoke said, "I am disappointed, but I still appreciate the drink and honesty, old-timer. Much obliged." And with that, he swung himself into his saddle and kept on riding.

The next day another young wrangler came riding into town on the very trail and from the direction the previous cowboy had. He made his way to the saloon, tied up his mount, and walked in to find rest and a cold, frosty pint. He leaned up against the bar and ordered a drink. After a sip, he turned to the bartender and asked, "Pardon me, sir, but what sort of folks live here in this town?"

The old man casually walked over, leaned against the bar opposite the young cowpuncher, looked him in the eye, and asked, "Well, young fella, what were those folks like in the town you just came from?"

The young cattleman looked out the window for a moment and then back at the old man, shook his head, and with a reflective, easy smile, wistfully said, "Alas, they were the best I ever met. The most hardworking and honest folk that you could trust. They would give ya the shirt off their back if you needed it. A most unselfish lot as there ever was. The ranch I was at was overstaffed and, sadly, me being the greenie, they had to let me go. That is why I am here, looking for a new gig in a new town."

The old bartender smiled broadly and said, "Well, young fella, you're in luck. You'll find the same kinda folk in this town. Perhaps I can introduce you to a few local ranchers who are looking for help."

Authors and researchers Rodd Wagner and Gale Muller sum it up this way: "The world you inhabit is the world you make. Your reputation precedes you, biasing the way new colleagues deal with you. Your first moves, friendly or hostile, tip the balance for future interactions. When you exhibit trust, you will most often find trustworthiness. When you are selfish, you will most often find selfishness. When you compete, others must resort to competition. If you choose to play the game strictly for your advantage, your attempts at collaboration will indeed be (as Thomas Hobbes said), 'solitary, poor, nasty, brutish, and short.'"[3]

As I mentioned earlier, truth, authenticity, and vulnerability start with you. That means you decide how others will view and treat you based on how you view and treat others. If you want to connect, put yourself in a position to be connected with. Do the things others will be attracted to. Look them in the eye and communicate with honest vulnerability. Sometimes that honesty is not fun. Sometimes it can be perceived as harsh and painful, but more often than not it will be dressed in love, sincerity, and a desire to actually connect.

As we move forward, I am going to tell many stories. I feel compelled to say that as important as storytelling is, I believe it's more important to be a "story holder." You must bask in the light of others and allow them to share from time to time. You must give them the emotional space and comfort that allows them to drop their mask and talk to you. Rachel Naomi Remen taught, "The most basic and powerful way to connect to another person is to listen. Just listen. Perhaps the most important thing we ever give each other is our attention. . . . A loving silence often has far more power to heal and to connect than the most well-intentioned words."[4] You must listen to your friends' stories and savor and celebrate their authenticity and empathize with their pain. Hold their stories with reverence. Let your friends know you can be trusted and are worthy of hearing their stories. And when appropriate, laugh with them.

We should take every opportunity to laugh with each other. I mean really belly laugh, set aside our egos, and just chill out. If we did this instead of engaging in anger and physical altercations when emotions get heated and battle lines are drawn, this world would be a far better place. Why do we get so fixated on our own perspective and believe that we have all the answers when the reality is that we are all seeking truth, happiness, and connectedness with each other?

I know birds of a feather flock together, and we enjoy associating with others who see the world as we see it. But I submit that you just may find inner peace and contentment you've never experienced if you soften your heart, open your mind, hang out with, and allow yourself to listen to someone who does not see the world as you see it.

I wish we could set our egos, traditions, and perceptions aside. I wish we could all take a softer approach with those who do not see politics or religion as we do and strive to learn, understand, and entertain that with which we disagree. Instead, many are fixed in their way of thinking and believe they hold the only facts. These people are often mystified as to why others do not see things the way they do.

When these people cannot convert you into thinking and believing as they think and believe, they experience pain, frustration, and sadness. These negative emotions can grow into alienation, anger, and hatred. And guess what? Love and connectedness cannot thrive under those conditions.

Instead, we must learn to be more empathetic with one another. That means we must learn to laugh, love, and live in this world as brothers and sisters of the human race. To live a rich, full life, you must open your mind and heart to the perspectives of others. You must love those who are different *because* of their differences. Real love does not have the luxury of picking and choosing who is deserving of its tenderness, adoration, and acceptance.

Unconditional love is unconditional. Acceptance can heal deep wounds. And laughter is a balm for the soul. And on that note, let's dive into the *L*'s face-first!

—— § ——

CHAPTER 1

Laughing: The Best of Times
Even in the Worst of Times

"Laughter is the shortest distance between two people."
—*Victor Borge*

ONE OF THE EASIEST and best ways to connect with someone else is also one of the simplest—laugh! That's right. Without even realizing it, the second you let out anything from a giggle to a full-blown belly laugh, you send a series of powerful messages to the people you're with: You accept them. You like them. You want to be with them. Laughter is just about the best medicine any family or relationship can have on hand. I know beyond a shadow of doubt that humor is vitally important to living a life full of love and joy. Humor is also a great way to get to know someone's true personality.

It was Russian novelist and philosopher Fyodor Dostoyevsky who said, "If you wish to glimpse inside a human soul and get to know a man, don't bother analyzing his ways of being silent, of talking, of weeping, of seeing how much he is moved by noble ideas; you will get better results if you just watch him laugh. If he laughs well, he's a good man."[5] Dostoyevsky's profound statement substantiates that laughter is an important emotional expression.

You undoubtedly know how our ability to communicate laughter has evolved right along with our technological prowess. Think of all the ways you're able to convey laughter in the various forms of media today: laughing memes, smiley or laughing-face emojis, and the standard LOL or LMAO. But nothing replaces the addictive, smile-inducing giggle of a face-to-face, friend-to-friend, sincere belly laugh.

Before we really dive into the joys and benefits of laughter, I want to make sure we're on the same page. Laughter is a sword that can cut both ways. Here's what I mean: Most of the time, laughter is a positive, fun, robust way to enjoy life. But, sadly, laughter can sometimes be negative. There's a big difference between laughing *with* and laughing *at* others, and you intuitively know the difference when you see it, feel it, or experience it. There are a couple of reasons why cruel-hearted people laugh at others. They may be doing it to make themselves feel better. Or they may be trying to make others conform to their way of thinking. At its worst, it's a total put-down of someone else.

Whatever the reason for laughing *at* others, it's a sure way to ostracize them. In that case, laughter divides, separates, and isolates. That's *not* the kind of laughter we'll be discussing in this chapter. When you laugh *with* others, it draws you closer and forms strong bonds of love, friendship, and connectedness. And that's the kind of laughter we're going to explore here.

A Universal Language of Connection

There are about 6,500 languages spoken on the earth today— and the thing they all share is laughter. Laughter is a worldwide form of interaction that connects all humans. It's something we all recognize, appreciate, and welcome. And we're all born with the capacity to laugh! Unlike even our native tongue—whether that be English, Mandarin, Russian, or even sign language—we don't have to learn to laugh.

Laughter is one of a baby's first forms of communication. Babies start to laugh at about three to four months of age, long before they can speak. Just like crying, laughter is a way for an infant to communicate—the way a baby says "I love you. I feel safe with you. I trust you. I feel connected to you." Nothing melts a parent's heart more than a baby's first laugh.

If you've spent any time around children, you know that they laugh freely and often. There are no reliable studies that put a number on how often people of different ages laugh, but we do know one thing for sure: children laugh much more often—and with greater intensity—than adults do. Maybe we adults get too preoccupied with the mortgage and income taxes and our upcoming physical exam. Or maybe we simply lose our interest and aptitude for humorous, good-hearted play. What a shame! We need to laugh more for many reasons.

One of those reasons is that laughter means good times. I'd like you to take a quick stroll down memory lane. Think of the best times you've ever had with your family. Without even knowing your particular memory, I'm betting that some good, hearty laughter was involved. For me, one of the best times in my family history has to be the time I ran around with a pair of underpants on my head to entertain my kids—but more about that later.

Along with forming a solid connection between people, laughter has the powerful ability to turn what eleven-year-old Alexander would call "a terrible, horrible, no good, very bad day"[6] into material for a comedy routine, just like that. You've seen it—things can be going terribly wrong, but the second someone erupts in laughter, everything is suddenly right. Whether we realize it or not, we all have plenty of comic material oozing out of our pores. And, best of all, those of us who can laugh at themselves will never stop being amused.

An excellent example of this is when educator and author John-Roger was traveling with some friends on the lecture circuit. When they finally arrived at their destination, the plane was late. That was annoying. *Really* annoying. To make matters worse, their luggage was the last to drop onto the conveyor belt. You got it—that was even worse. And when their luggage finally *did* appear, one piece was damaged. Another of their suitcases had sprung open, splaying clothing and personal items—uh-huh, some were *very* personal—all over the conveyor belt. It's not hard to visualize. The people in John-Roger's group were becoming increasingly upset. Hot under the collar, to put it mildly. A few were catapulting toward rage.

Finally, John-Roger turned to the group and said, "Relax. This is funny. A few weeks from now we'll be telling stories about this and laughing about it. If it'll be funny then, it's funny now." Just like magic, everything changed. They started looking at their situation as if it were a Woody Allen movie. When some of the luggage didn't show up at all, they smiled. When the car-rental agency totally blew off their reservation and they were left without transportation, they laughed. And when they heard there was a taxi strike, they *howled* with laughter.

Mark Twain once said that "against the assault of laughter, nothing can stand."[7] Our group of intrepid travelers with roughed-up luggage and no way to reach their hotel are proof.

So exactly where do laughter and a sense of humor come from? Do you think they're lurking somewhere along our genetic strands? I've met lots of people who seem to have been cheated when humor was doled out in our DNA. Or maybe we all start with strong funny bones that atrophy as we go through the hardships and trials of life. And just maybe there are people who don't feel worthy of laughter and joy.

I tend to think that laughter and humor are a combination of our intrinsic genetic makeup and learned behavior. You probably know people who suffer from poor learned behavior: they take life way too seriously. They have a permanent scowl. They recoil at the silliness of others—as if laughter is at odds with their need to maintain constant sobriety. They seem almost afraid to show others their silly side. *What if no one laughs? What if they don't find my humor funny? Heavens to Betsy, I may come off looking vulnerable, weak, or even stupid.* So they screw on their mask of seriousness even more tightly. After all, it will protect them.

I hope that doesn't describe you! We all get grumpy now and then, but sometimes if we're not paying attention, we can allow negative feelings to hijack our mood for days or weeks. Time to ask yourself some serious questions: Do I have a laughter deficiency? Am I humor impaired? Am I too often holding a glass that's half empty? Do I skulk about with a pout or scowl on my face? If so, then you *really* need to digest what I'm about to share!

When we're sucked up in the tornado of life's trials, adversities, and challenges, it's not always easy to stop and lighten the mood with humor. Life can be a bitch, and things don't always go our way. I get it. I've been there; you've been there. We've all been there!

During those excruciatingly painful moments in my life, even in the midst of the shit storms, I recognized I had a choice: I could break down and cry, or I could pause, step back, look at the bright side, and try to laugh at the situation. Sure, I admit I occasionally shed massive alligator tears. But more often than not, I tried to choose the path of joy. Marjorie Pay Hinckley, a venerable woman in her late eighties, said it best: "The only way to get through life is to laugh your way through it. You either have to laugh or cry. I prefer to laugh. Crying gives me a headache."[8]

Finding the humor in every situation really does help alleviate stress. But there's even more to it than that. Laughing makes us feel good, and that good feeling stays with us even after the laughter is long gone. Laughing helps us realize that our challenges in life are not the earth-shattering, cataclysmic events we often make them out to be. Laughing helps us look at those challenges from a different perspective; our woes seem far less grave, and our minds and hearts are opened to increased objectivity and insight. And let me share a secret: both sadness and joy are highly contagious. Few things on this planet are as infectious as pure joy, laughter, and good humor. In fact, we often laugh at the sound of laughter itself.

While you may be trying to deliberately look on the bright side of things, most laughter is spontaneous and unrehearsed. It almost always erupts involuntarily. As humans, we can suppress laughter, and we can fake laughter, but it is very difficult— even hopeless—to intentionally create *sincere laughter*.

Have you ever tried to laugh on command? It's next to impossible! If you don't believe me, go ahead and conduct a little test: ask a friend to laugh on demand. He may make the sounds. His face may exhibit the expression of laughter, but you'll be able to see in a heartbeat just how phony and contrived it is. Of course, you may end up genuinely laughing at how ridiculous you both look and sound while trying to force laughter.

Sincere laughter can't be faked. Others see right through it. That's why genuine laughter is one of the most essential ingredients of forming deep human connections. We can trust a sincere laugh. We know it's real. We know it's authentic. Laughter offers others a genuine, unedited view of our character. Laughter is a pure, dependable demonstration that erupts from deep within and tells others "I like you, I want you to like me, and I want to connect with you."

Most everyone reading this book has been on a date or dating website. When we are looking for those we want to partner with, laughter is often the most important variable in this partner-vetting process. Why? You cannot pretend. You are either saying "I like you, I want you to like me, and I want to connect with you," or you are not. Think back to the first time you and your partner met. I can assure you there was plenty of good-natured laughter that forged that connection. I submit that without real laughter there can be no real lasting love. Just as moisture grants life to plants, laughter gives life to love, so water your relationships daily.

Situational Science

This may surprise you, but research shows that most laughter is not the result of a joke someone intentionally tells. In fact, most of the time laughter is a response to a situation that's not even meant to be funny. That's right—far more laughter takes place during normal, daily interaction with friends, family, and colleagues. Laughter is much more often about shared behavior where we demonstrate to others that we like, understand, and want to connect with them.

Here's a perfect example. One Saturday morning, my then-six-year-old daughter, Kelly, grabbed the milk out of the refrigerator, held the carton in one hand while putting her other hand on her hip, looked directly at my wife and me sitting at the kitchen table, and in total soberness (perhaps even a bit of a snotty attitude) asked, "What is the date on this milk?" She wasn't trying to be funny. I think she honestly wanted to know when the milk expired. But her behavior struck us as being so odd we both burst out in laughter.

In cases like Kelly and the milk, we don't deliberately decide to laugh. Our brain automatically decides for us. These seemingly insignificant, spontaneous, small chuckles and deep belly laughs are key components of the loving, connecting ties that bind our relationships. And everyone enjoys a good laugh!

As our experience with Kelly shows, laughter is also highly contagious. One of my favorite movies of all time is Walt Disney's *Mary Poppins*. One of the songs in the movie is "I Love to Laugh." It's sung by Uncle Albert (Ed Wynn) as he levitates uncontrollably toward the ceiling. At first, Mary Poppins (Julie Andrews) tries to disapprove of Uncle Albert's silly behavior. But before long the comically contagious incident sends Mary, Bert (Dick Van Dyke), and the Banks children into the air. They are pulled upward simply because those around them are giggling, hissing, and laughing like dental patients on laughing gas.

The symbolism is powerful: laughter can kick off positive thoughts and feelings that lighten the mood and put things into perspective. So how did they all get down again? They simply thought about sad things. Again, the symbolism is compellingly thought-provoking. Think sad thoughts, be the victim, wallow in self-pity, and you will bring yourself and those around you down.

You know how much fun laughing is. What you might not believe is that laughter is good for your health. That's right. Those folks who said, "Laughter is the best medicine" were spot on. And that's not just my opinion. There's a lot of science to back it up. When it comes right down to it, though, we and our sophisticated scientific theories are pretty late in the game. The connection between laughter and good health was recognized years and years ago. One thirteenth-century surgeon told jokes to his patients as they emerged from operations. A sixteenth-century British physician prescribed laughter for people with head colds and depression; a favorite "cure" was being tickled in the armpits. (Can you just imagine your physician lunging at you, headed straight for your pits? That alone should bring on a good guffaw or two!)

Ancient Ojibway Indian doctor clowns, aka Windigokan, used laughter to heal the sick. In fact, some American Indian tribes—the Zunis, Crees, Pueblos, and Hopis among them—had ceremonial clowns whose sole purpose it was to provide humor for their tribesmen. They were called in to heal the sick with their hilarity, frightening away the demons of ill health. (I'm asking here that you suspend your belief for a minute and realize that this was back in the day when clowns were *funny*, not *creepy*.) Speaking of clowns, famous seventeenth-century physician Thomas Sydenham said that "the arrival of a good clown exercises more beneficial influence upon the health of a town than twenty asses laden with drugs."[9] And *that's* a lot of drugs (and a lot of asses when you think about it).

So what's the actual scientific benefit of laughter? There are several good reasons why laughing is so good for your health. For one thing, according to Laughter Online University, it boosts your immunity, helping you resist infections and fight the ones you do have.[10] It increases energy, relieves pain, reduced stress, and simply makes you feel good.

Healing Humor

One of the top experts on laughter as medicine is former *Saturday Review* editor Norman Cousins. He speaks from personal experience. Suffering from a debilitating and often fatal connective-tissue disease, he used funny books and movies to help relieve his pain. He reported that ten minutes of genuine belly laughing worked better than anesthesia and gave him hours of pain-free sleep.

Finally healed from his disease, Cousins became an advocate for laughter as medicine and took his show on the road. One of his favorite experiences was at a veterans' hospital with a group of cancer patients. They were mighty glum, as you may suspect. Still, Cousins described the benefits of laughter and challenged the sixty men to infuse some humor and good cheer into their lives. He promised to come back in a few weeks to see how they were doing.

When Cousins returned to the hospital a few weeks later, he immediately saw impressive changes. In their meeting that morning, each veteran was asked to tell about something good that had happened to him since the previous meeting. As each one told about something good, intermittent cheering burst forth from the others. Talk about connecting!

When all had taken a turn, they turned to face Cousins. Obviously, they expected him to relate a story as well. And he had a great one.

"What I have to report is better than good," he said. "It's wonderful. Actually, it's better than wonderful. It's unbelievable. And as long as I live, I don't expect that anything as magnificent as this can possibly happen to me again."

The veterans leaned forward in their seats, anticipating a total connection with Cousins.

"When I arrived at the Los Angeles airport last Wednesday, my bag was the first off the carousel."

An eruption of applause and acclaim greeted this announcement.

"I had never even *met* anyone whose bag was first off the carousel," he continued. There were more loud expressions of delight. He had connected, all right—they could all relate to *that*.

"Flushed with success, I went to the nearest telephone to report my arrival to my office. [Oh, the travails of the days before cell phones.] That was when I lost my coin. I pondered this melancholy event for a moment, or two then decided to report it to the operator.

"Operator," he said, "I put a quarter in and didn't get my number. The machine kept my coin."

"Sir," she said, "if you give me your name and address, we'll mail the coin to you."

Cousins was appalled.

"Operator, why don't you just return my coin and let's be friends."

"Sir," she repeated in a flat voice, "if you give me your name and address, we will mail you the refund."

Then, almost by way of afterthought, she asked, "Sir, did you remember to press the coin return plunger?"

Truth be told, Cousins had overlooked this nicety. He pressed the plunger. To his great surprise, it worked. In fact, it was apparent that the machine had been badly constipated and he happened to have the laxative. All at once, the vitals of the machine opened up and proceeded to spew out coins of almost every denomination. The profusion was so great that he had to use his empty hand to contain the overflow.

The noise, of course, could be heard over the telephone and was not lost on the operator.

"Sir," she asked, "what is happening?"

He reported that the machine had just given up all its earnings of at least the past few months.

"Sir," she said, "please put the coins back in the box."

"Operator," he said, "if you give me your name and address, I will be glad to mail you the coins."[11]

According to Cousins, the veterans "exploded with cheers. David triumphs over Goliath. At the bottom of the ninth inning, with the home team behind by three runs, the weakest hitter in the lineup hits the ball out of the park. A mammoth business corporation is brought to its knees. Every person who has been exasperated by the loss of a coin in a public telephone booth could identify with my experience and share both in the triumph of justice and the humiliation of the mammoth and the impersonal oppressor."[12] It was a solid, foolproof connection, and everyone in the room felt it.

One of the doctors in the room, noticing how relaxed and mobile the men were, asked how many had been experiencing their usual pain when they arrived at the meeting. More than half raised their hands. The doctor then asked how many noticed that their pain had receded or completely disappeared. The same hands went up.

Laughing also has tremendous psychological benefits. In addition to forging healthy connections between people, laughing and having a humorous outlook on life enhances self-esteem, promotes creativity, improves negotiating and decision-making skills, maintains a sense of balance, improves performance, bestows a sense of power, relieves stress, and improves coping abilities. That's a whole lot of bang for the buck, and we can all use that. Comedian Red Skelton said, "No matter what your heartache may be, laughing helps you forget it for a few seconds."[13]

And here's one of the best parts: the physiological changes that happen during laughter are so radical that laughter may be classified as aerobic activity. You got it—quite literally, it's a form of *internal jogging*. Even if you're not into running a mile every day or working out at the gym, *this* is an exercise you can get into. It's simple. It requires no special training, no special equipment. You don't have to do it at the gym or on the track or on a Nautilus machine. All you need is a sense of humor and something to laugh at. And face it—those things are all around!

A guy named Robert Brody described the physiology of laughter in an article in *American Health* magazine. Take a look, and you'll see why it's a total inner-body workout.

First, something you see or hear or even think about sets off "a massive brain reaction." The nerve fibers throughout your body trigger a snowballing cycle of discharges in your brain stem. News flash: something is funny.

Electrical and chemical impulses then wash through the frontal lobes of your brain, go to its motor centers, and land smack in the center of your cerebral cortex. The cortex then hands an order to your body: Laugh!

This is where the fun really starts. The muscles in your face that control expression start to contort. You almost lapse into a grimace. Muscles throughout your body contract like fists. Your vocal-cord muscles, designed for intelligible sound, cannot co-ordinate. Your throat opens, relaxed and ready to vibrate. Your diaphragm tenses up in anticipation of respiratory spasms. You feel pressure building in your lungs. (At this point, Brody says, "Trying to hold in a laugh is no less than a violation against nature—rarely successful."[14])

Once the laugh gets into full gear, your breathing is inter-rupted for a station break. Your lower jaw vibrates. A blast of air gusts into your throat, flinging mucus against the walls of your windpipe. Pandemonium! Out comes your laugh, in some cases clocked at an astonishing 170 miles an hour. You issue a strange machine-gun sound, almost a violent bark.

Once in the throes of a full-bodied laugh, your body bucks. Your torso flexes. Your arms flap and your hands slap your thighs. Your eyes squeeze out tears. You puff and rasp in as much rhythm as a symphony. As Brody sums it up, "You can hardly stand so much glee coursing through you. You're wobbly in the knees, wheezing like an asthmatic. Pleading for mercy, you collapse on the nearest sofa. Sounds like fun, no?"[15]

It *is* fun, and in our family, we love it. Some of our best laughs result when I tell my kids stories from my youth. I love the connection it forges between us, and they just love to hear some hilarious stuff about good old Dad. Some—okay, many—are embarrassing. Some have morals. Others are just funny and make my kids laugh. The ones that bring the greatest laughs seem to be the ones where I demonstrated the greatest stupidity. Lucky for my kids, I have plenty of material to draw from. Surprising though it may seem, I did some mind-bogglingly stupid things as a kid.

Recalling the Silly Stupidity of Our Youth

You probably have some funny stories from your glory days in your repertoire. You know the kind: sliding down the stairway handrail (something that rarely ends the way you envision). Toilet papering the neighbor's house. Water ballooning another car and its occupants (which is illegal, by the way). Jumping off the roof with a blanket as a parachute. Building a miniature cannon in metal shop and using it to shoot a steel marble through the backyard fence. Need I go on?

Examples of the stupid things I did are almost endless, but a few stick out in my mind—and they still make me (and my kids) laugh because of the unbelievable stupidity of my escapades. Once I shot my brother's best friend with my BB gun from two hundred feet. That's not an easy task when you consider that I was shooting from my bedroom window through a screen. I remember aiming relatively high to compensate for the pathetically weak velocity and arching trajectory.

It worked! The BB hit the kid right on his bare calf. He yelped. When my brother asked what was wrong, I heard his friend say, "A bee stung me!" Can you just hear me snickering?

That little bit of success inspired another even more mischievous idea. We lived near a swim and tennis club. And, of course, I'd noticed that the fence near the diving board had knotholes in it—perfect for sighting in on unsuspecting divers. Plunk, plunk, plunk, and guess what? They too thought they had been stung by bees. (I should mention here that I never got caught. The only reason I dare write about it now is that I feel confident I have exceeded the statute of limitations on committing a crime with a pathetically weak Red Rider Daisy BB gun.)

It didn't stop there—because, of course, I had more weapons in my arsenal than my BB gun. I had a great bow-and-arrow set. I liked to go to the high ridges overlooking Deep Cliff, the local golf course. But don't panic. I wasn't shooting anyone with my bow and arrows. No, what I did was fairly innocent, but it provided me with hours of laughter.

Here's how it went down: I would meticulously tie a fire-cracker between the fletchings on one of my arrows. Then I'd light the fuse and let the arrow fly, timing the impact so it hit the green just as the golfers were strolling up the fairway toward their little white balls. The golfers would see the arrow land and stop in their tracks, puzzled. Next thing they knew, BANG! CRACK! That's when they *really* got nervous. And not a few fled in terror.

The golfers never figured out where the arrows were coming from, and I always managed a clean, fast getaway, so I never got in trouble for that one, either.

I wasn't so lucky with one of my other schemes. I grew up with four sisters. My sister just younger than I was always had her dates pick her up at the house. Every time, my brother and I were waiting on the roof. I was always armed with my BB gun and bow and arrow.

For the initial assault, I would launch an arrow or two into the front lawn next to the steps that led to the front door. If that didn't scare them off, I popped them with my BB gun. More than one scampered back to the car, drove off, and called the house from the pay phone down at the corner 7-Eleven (another inconvenience before the invention of cell phones).

I can still hear my mother yelling from the front porch. "AAAARRRRRTHUR FERRELL COOOOOOMBS THE THIRD, get down from that roof this very instant!" I could always gauge my mother's level of sincerity by the names she used for me. Full name equaled full rage. My little brother and I would scurry down off the roof. When the nervous suitor reappeared, my mother would make us apologize. We did, of course, but the laughs we got were well worth it.

Sometimes I tremble to think of the stupid things I did in search of laughs. At one point, I brilliantly invented a game called "Who Can Get Closest without Getting Hit?" Even the name itself made me chuckle then, though it fills me with chagrin now.

Here's how it worked: My younger brother and I would take my bow and arrows to the local high school football field. (Brief time out: I need to make sure you understand that my brother was a more-than-willing participant.)

Each of us would then stand on the fifty-yard line, and I would load an arrow in the bow. I'd pull the string all the way back with my three middle fingers. Aiming straight into the air, I'd shoot the arrow directly over our heads as if I were some medieval archer. The arrow would fly fast at first, but as it reached its aeronautical apex, it would slow until it paused, appearing to be suspended midair. Then it would slowly turn and begin its tortuous descent to the earth. The closer it got, the faster it seemed to fall.

As soon as I'd shot the arrow, I would drop the bow, and my brother and I would start wrestling for position. (You see where this is going? Insane, right?) We pushed, shoved, boxed, and grappled each other to see who could get closest to the falling arrow when it pierced the ground without getting hit. You lost if your opponent was closer than you. You also lost if you got struck by the falling projectile. (Even though it was a target-practice arrow, it would still injure you if it hit you.)

Just writing about it makes me shudder. How stupid could two teenage boys be?

I am happy to report that the arrows never hit either of us. But I am embarrassed to say there were plenty of times I danced around like a fool and celebrated when the arrow embedded itself several inches into the ground literally inches from me. As a young idiot, I never once stopped to think what could have happened had the arrow actually hit one of us.

I am also happy to report that I've had *plenty* of experiences since then that have made me—and the people around me—laugh without involving danger. I love those times! I especially love it when the laughter involves my kids, because it's a sweet connection we share, even when I'm teaching them lessons about what *NOT* to do using my crazy stories as examples. I also love it because children who learn to laugh at certain situations are much more capable of coping with the curveballs life will certainly throw them as they grow older. And I know those curveballs will eventually fly toward my kids.

Having a pleasant sense of humor is far more essential than having the talent to tell a couple of funny jokes or the ability to pull an occasional prank. It's a state of mind that permits you to see the sunnier side of life. Humor acts as a lens, allowing us to change our reality and help us manage stressful events.

Recognizing and embracing the sillier stuff in life makes it a bit easier to cope with tough times.

A healthy sense of humor is a vital ingredient for a child in building strong self-esteem. People with a healthy sense of humor are typically more popular and form friendships more easily. In turn, they usually feel better about themselves and those in their social circles.

And that's not all: a child who can laugh at himself when he makes a mistake has an easier time accepting imperfection and is less afraid to try again.

The Adventures of Underwear Man

Helping my kids develop a great sense of humor brings me to the pair of underpants on my head. You see, I love wrestling with and tickling my kids. On Saturday mornings, I slide into their beds and tickle their backs. That leads to more tickling, which in turn often leads to massive wrestling matches. And all of it is punctuated with plenty of side-splitting laughter.

That whole wrestling image sparked an idea one morning. I took a pair of clean underwear, put it on my head, and positioned the leg holes over my eyes. I looked like a very bad, cheesy, 1970s professional wrestler. I gave myself the theatrical name of "Underwear Man."

I stood around the corner of the room where my kids were playing. Still out of sight, I did my best imitation of a ring announcer and yelled, "ARE YOOOOU READY TOOOO RUUUUMBLE?!" As soon as I heard them giggle, I stepped out.

The giggling turned to screams of laughter as they saw me with the underwear pulled tightly over my head. One cried, "Dad, your nose is right where the crotch is! Gross!"

To that I replied, "I AM UNDEERRRWEEEEAAAR MAAAAN! NOOOO ONE DARES TO CHALLENGE ME!" I then stood on the coffee table flexing and posing, theatrically mimicking a professional wrestler. The more I hammed it up, the harder they laughed.

After some very melodramatic moves, we started to wrestle. I picked my kids up and gently slammed them on the couch. I jumped on them and pretended to get the count from the ref, and I dramatically fell off the couch just before the imaginary ref called the match over.

My—and my kids'—favorite move was what I called the double-fisted pile driver. I would pin them on their backs on the couch, plant my fists on their chests, and made short, shaking movements that jiggled and vibrated their entire bodies. They'd laugh hysterically.

After that, Underwear Man was a regular guest in our home. We all loved the way we could turn a regular old sofa or bed into a high-stakes wrestling arena for a laughter-filled match we all enjoyed.

One Saturday, as I was working in the garage, I came into the house and heard some whispering and giggling. My kids were playing downstairs with neighborhood friends, and my parental radar detected that they were excited and wanted me to come downstairs. I didn't know what I was in for, but the anticipation for them was palpable.

As I made my way downstairs, the whispering and giggling increased. As I turned the corner at the bottom of the stairs, I saw seven kids ranging from five to ten years old, all with underwear pulled over their heads, calling me out in a ferocious challenge.

Never one to shy away from a wrestling match, I jumped in and took them on. I got one or two pinned on the couch when the others jumped on my back, screaming, "I will save you!" The two I had pinned scrambled out and escaped. I then crumbled from the weight, regained my composure, pulled the kids off my back, and pinned them, only to have two more jump on my back so the pinned ones could escape. We all laughed like hyenas!

This old grappler—the original Underwear Man—was way outnumbered. But the laughter of children has always been one of the sweetest sounds I know. Nothing can bring you closer to heaven than to hear a child laugh. And nothing can bring you closer to your kids than sharing that laugh.

The Case of the Mistaken Airport Identity

Another of my more hilarious episodes involved my neighbors, the Abbotts. Milo and Boon Abbott live around the corner from us. We love their family. I have always had a soft spot in my heart for these young men. They are truly authentic—no pretense, hypocrisy, or judgment of others.

One day I was on my way to San Diego on a business trip. Because of my crazy travel schedule, I have been prescreened by TSA for a while now—it's one of the little perks that make frequent flying a bit easier.

While standing in my short line, I glanced over at the long line of people who had to half undress only to have some TSA dude ask them to hold their hands over their head so a truly revealing image could be scanned.

Lo and behold, who did I see in that other line?

Boon Abbott!

It wasn't tough to spot him. You can't mistake his tall frame, Abbott family features, and blond, curly hair. As I whizzed by, he was just behind me, waiting for his items to come through the X-ray machine on the conveyor belt. He didn't see me, so I waited a few seconds while he gathered his stuff. He grabbed his backpack, shoes, and belt and walked over to the benches just beyond the TSA body-scan machines but not past the TSA tower overlooking the entire operation.

I watched as he slipped his shoes on and waited for his family; I figured they must be in the sea of travelers still lined up for body scans. While he stood and started threading his belt through his pants, I decided to have a little fun. After all, I rarely pass up the opportunity to play a good-hearted practical joke.

I quietly and nonchalantly sneaked up behind him. (Remember, there were TSA agents, airport security, and police everywhere—not exactly a great place to draw attention by skulking about.) Once behind him, I quickly threw my arms around him, pinning him firmly. Being an old wrestler, I knew all the right moves: I locked the grip tight, squeezed, and lifted him. (You ancient wrestling friends can probably feel this sensation and movement without even giving it conscious thought.)

I hoisted him easily and, having pinned his arms, lifted his feet four to five inches off the ground. He was completely immobile.

But I couldn't stop there. Upping the ante, I tucked my chin into the middle of his back and applied a little pressure. At that point, it was next to impossible for him to turn and see me. I bounced him a few times, and in a disguised, gruff, smoker's sort of voice, I said, "You do not know who's got you, do you? You have no idea who I am, do you?" I could just imagine Boon's mind spinning with possibilities. He'd probably realize it was me in just a few seconds since our families are so close and he's seen me wrestle with my kids often. And I'd probably see the rest of his family come through the line any minute now. We'd all have a good laugh and then be off to our respective gates.

He tried to wiggle and turn, but my deep, viselike grip made resistance futile. I heard him start to laugh nervously. With that, I let him down after giving him one more quick squeeze. I had a huge grin on my face as Boon turned to face me.

At that moment I was stunned.

HOLY CRAP—it wasn't Boon Abbott!

The strange young man—who couldn't have been more than fourteen—looked at me and said with a face devoid of all emotion, "You're right, sir. I didn't know who had me."

I was speechless. Utterly dumbfounded. And more than a little horrified! With eyes still wide in shock, I finally managed to stammer, "Well, I have to run now and catch my flight. See ya later." I fled down the terminal toward my gate, praying I wouldn't be arrested for tackling a stranger near airport security.

The poor kid just stood there in a daze.

Halfway down the terminal, I partly expected a protective dad to tackle me as his wife, in hot pursuit, screamed, "Stop that old letch!" I pictured them stuck behind the wall of security watching the scene unfold, wondering who I was and what I was doing to their son. I wondered if I should duck into a bathroom until they called my flight for the last time. Instead, I raced to the gate as fast as I could. *Heavens to Betsy, I'm an idiot!* I thought to myself.

I could just hear their conversations: "Hey, son, who was that old guy wrestling with you near security?" "Mom, I have no freaking idea. The creep just came up and bear-hugged me and started whispering in my ear."

Or perhaps the Boon lookalike had reported me to Salt Lake International Airport security. I could just hear that as well: "Hey, some strange, old, gray-haired, smoker-voiced man is grabbing young boys in the airport. I have no clue who he is."

But to my profound relief, no one came for me.

Once at the gate, I panicked. What if this kid and his family were also going to San Diego? What if they were on my flight? All the while I was half laughing at what I had done and was freaked out at the same time.

Once the plane door shut and we were in the air, I laughed and laughed. In fact, I laughed all the way to San Diego. I also swore to myself that I would never tackle a stranger again. That was too close a call, all in the name of getting a laugh.

I still wonder what stories the boy is telling. Maybe he is now seeing a therapist. Or maybe a sketchy, penciled image of me is floating around airport security. Who knows.

Perhaps I should be less impetuous. Perhaps I should stop teasing and playing silly jokes on others. But some positive teasing, called *prosocial teasing,* has benefits. It can be playful, reveal affiliations, and help both the teaser and the teased feel closer and connected. I hope everyone I encounter knows that my teasing is meant to say "I love you, I know (or want to know) you, and you're one of mine."

The Holy Humorous Trinity

My wrestle with the strange boy in the airport was an unfortunate case of mistaken identity. I'll never forget another uproarious mistake in our family—this one of mistaken meaning. It stemmed from a struggle with another language. I love H. Jackson Brown Jr.'s motto: "Never make fun of someone who speaks broken English. It means they know another language." While that reminder applies here, this example does warrant a snicker or two.

The riotous experience I'm remembering happened while I was trying to learn Dutch. My family and I lived in Holland for more than seven years, but my Dutch was and still is embarrassingly pathetic. That doesn't mean I didn't try. Trust me—Dutch is no easy language to learn. At least it wasn't for me. As a family, we tried hard to learn the language—and because of our efforts, we won the hearts of many Dutch friends who admired our willingness to attempt to make those throaty noises sound normal.

My wife at the time was far better and braver than I was. She often put herself in situations that forced her to speak Dutch on a more regular basis.

I was stunned when she announced that she was going to be teaching Sunday school to the children in a local church congregation we attended. Sure, there were a few expat kids scattered about, but by and large, most of the youth were authentically Dutch and spoke very little, if any, English. What a brave, brave soul she was. It is hard enough holding the attention of small children when you speak their mother tongue fluently, so her accepting this teaching opportunity was a true test of faith.

My wife exemplified what a caring, hardworking, kind Sunday school teacher is all about. Each week she painstakingly prepared, practiced, and fretted over her lesson. She worried all week about how to most effectively reach those impressionable, young Dutch minds. Most of the time, the kids quietly pondered her lesson and its meaning. Other times they laughed, giggled, and were entertained by my wife's message. This pattern continued for about a year.

One Sunday morning, one of the Dutch mothers approached us as we were about to drive home from church. She humbly asked if she could speak to my wife about her lesson. This was nothing unusual; my wife often received praise from parents expressing their gratitude for her burgeoning bilingual ability and how she was genuinely reaching the children in a powerful way. My young daughter Kelly and I kept walking toward the car to give them some privacy. Once at the car, we waited for their conversation to run its course.

I watched from a distance as the conversation progressed. As I watched, I could sense this was more than a passing accolade. I could tell by my wife's body language and facial expressions that something was wrong and that she was taking the woman's message very seriously. After several moments, they gave each other polite kisses on each cheek—the customary Dutch way of saying hello and good-bye to good friends—and my wife made her way to the car, where we were waiting.

I didn't have to even ask what the conversation was about; my wife was itching to tell me. In a hushed tone, so my young daughter could not hear and ask for definitions, my wife explained that she had been teaching the youth of that congregation the entire time about the Father, the Son, and the *Horny* Ghost.

Yes, you read that right.

We laughed uproariously all the way home. I *still* laugh about it.

All those times when those kids were giggling, snickering, and laughing, I thought my wife's wit was driving home some spiritual concept blended with a touch of humor. Not so. All year, my wife had been urging these kids to listen to and follow the Horny Ghost. She'd been telling them that the Horny Ghost would never lead them astray. I can only imagine the dinner conversations as well-meaning parents asked their innocent children, "So, what did you learn in Sunday school today?"

Never be scared of learning a new language. While learning anything new, especially a new language, nothing feels better than getting it right after getting it wrong.

What my wife taught me was that most everyone is essentially doing their best in this crazy, mixed-up world. No one is perfect; everybody has inner demons; everybody has flaws. Everyone is fighting a battle you know nothing about. Some of those battles revolve around incorrect translations.

When you watch others make mistakes as they are striving to learn, you will know they are in the arena of life, braving to lay it on the line. Learning, trying new things, and making mistakes go hand in hand. You cannot do one without the other. And it never hurts to soften the blow by laughing about it. Because in the end—just as with the Horny Ghost—it's likely to be pretty funny.

Batgirl, Bare Feet, and Contagious, Innocent Laughter

That leads me to another misspoken "mistake"—at least something I *thought* was about to be a huge mistake. It's something I remember to this day with a sidesplitting laugh.

I worked as a lifeguard at the Cupertino Hills Swim and Racket Club in my late teens and early twenties. I always had favorite swimmers, and one year it was the adorable, swim-like-a-freaking-fish, four-year-old Courtney. She wore a faded-blue Batgirl one-piece every day.

Courtney's mom dropped her off at the pool and then met up with other moms to play tennis. After tennis, Courtney's mom and her friends often sat at a nearby picnic table, enjoying a cold drink and chitchatting like young moms do. Yes, the other lifeguards and I joked that we were glorified day-care providers—but, oh, how I loved that job.

When Courtney's mom dropped her off at the pool, Courtney stood at the gate until she spotted me. Then, with a mischievous grin, she said in a singsong voice, "Arrrrrt, doooo noooot chaaaaase meeeee" (translation: *Art, please chase me*). On breaks, then, I dove in, swam under her, and tickled her like crazy. She giggled so hard I couldn't help but giggle along with her.

Whenever I sat in a regular chair instead of on the elevated lifeguard stand, Courtney occasionally sat in my lap and pretended to be a lifeguard. She wanted to blow my whistle and was the first to enforce pool rules—no running on the pool deck, only one jump on the diving board, stay out of the adult lap lanes, and so on. She also stood behind me as I sat on the deck and insisted on putting suntan lotion on my back and shoulders. She was such a good little buddy.

One day as the moms were finishing up, Courtney, who was sitting in my lap, said in a melodramatic way only a four-year-old can, "Art, this summer I have rubbed suntan lotion over your entiiiiiiiire body"—her arms gestured wide, and her voice grew louder to emphasize *entire*—"except one place."

Her mom, being a very good mom and having sonar hearing, immediately froze. So did the other moms. No one moved a muscle. They were speechless. They stared at Courtney and me. I could see them out of the corner of my eye. They appeared to be petrified as they deliberated their next move. *What should we do? Should we stop her? Where is this going? How will Art handle this?*

With a grin, I asked, "Courtney, what part of my body have you *not* rubbed suntan lotion on?" The moms' eyes grew wider as they all collectively sucked in a little air. I could tell they were about to intervene—or have massive heart attacks.

At that moment, Courtney turned and looked at me with the biggest, bluest eyes in the world and the funniest, you-have-got-to-be-kidding-me look on her face. She giggled as she said, "The bottom of your feet, silly."

What really made me laugh was the collective exhale from the moms, who had been about ready to implode. As the scene unfolded and the mothers heard and saw what transpired, even they started to chuckle in relief. I laughed and laughed and laughed some more, laughing until I couldn't laugh anymore. It still makes me laugh to this day.

You have to love the innocence of a child—so sweet, so tender, so priceless, and so angelic. A child's smile can brighten even the foulest of days. A child's innocence can charm the most cynical heart. What draws us to children and creates an instant soft spot in our hearts is not their physical beauty or their intrinsic sense of humor. The one thing we love most in children is the very thing we as adults have lost—innocence.

Is it possible to fully regain our childish innocence? I don't think so. But now that I am growing older, I occasionally sense my childlike innocence creeping up behind me. That sense of innocence is strongest while listening to my children laugh, watching the sun rise, standing on the beach and feeling the waves break against the shore, smelling the scent of a pine forest, or tasting cookie dough just before it's put in the oven.

Perhaps the secret of happiness and joy and laughter is letting your inner child enjoy the break from being an adult—that, and rubbing suntan lotion on the bottoms of your feet. The secret is also seeing the humor in every situation—and taking advantage of the opportunity to laugh.

While walking down the streets of Berlin one day, eighteenth-century philosopher Moses Mendelssohn accidentally collided with a plump Prussian officer. "Swine!" the officer bellowed. Mendelssohn, knowing that a reprisal would invite punishment from the officer, decided on a different approach—one laced with humor. He smiled, tipped his hat, and replied, "Mendelssohn." His reaction is proof that humor can turn any situation around.

And here's the good news: it's not too late to "learn" to have humor. Whenever you can, laugh with friends. It's true that laughter is contagious—and you're likely to laugh harder and longer with others than when you laugh alone. That's because while you're laughing, you're also connecting with someone.

If you want to have more fun in life, try following these suggestions of Leigh Anne Jasheway, coordinator of health promotion at the University of Texas Health Science Center at Houston:

Make a pledge to laugh out loud or to make someone else laugh out loud at least ten times everyday. As E.

E. Cummings said, "The most wasted of all days is one without laughter."

At least once a week, do something truly silly. And at least once a week, set aside time to call someone who always adds fun to your day.

Start a humor collection—you might collect jokes, clippings, cartoons, cards, mugs, books, or videos. Share funny things with others, too; try using stick-on notes with humorous messages.

Finally, try to find the humor in every predicament, because I guarantee you, it's there.

Perhaps one of the best suggestions is to create what author and stress-management expert Loretta LaRoche calls a "humor survival kit"—and one of her best tools in it, she says, always gets a laugh:

Buy something silly you can put on (a pair of Groucho Marx glasses are my favorite). Put them on in situations where you tend to awfulize. I wear mine driving through Boston, especially when I have to merge. People always let me in. Food shopping is another favorite. Among others, going to the dentist, the doctor, staff meetings, talking to your mate, the children, a coworker. When things have reached the limits of your endurance, go into a bathroom, look into the mirror, put on your glasses, and ask yourself this question: "How serious is this?"[16]

So lighten up. Be tender with yourself. Take it easy and relax. Accept life as it comes. Trust your inner spirit, and believe the best in life will find you. You are safe; learn to laugh, love, and live. You are not alone with your challenges. Everyone who has ever walked this earth has had challenges. So smile, stop worrying so much, laugh, be silly, and be happy. Appreciate and love this gift we call life.

Renowned American journalist Linda Ellerbee said, "I have always felt that laughter in the face of reality is probably the finest sound there is and will last until the day when the game is called on account of darkness. In this world, a good time to laugh is any time you can."[17]

Or, as legendary humorist Will Rogers advised, "We are all here for a spell. Get all the good laughs you can."

§

CHAPTER 2

Learning: Do It As If You Will Live Forever

"Learning is all about connections, and through our connections with unique people we are able to gain a true understanding of the world around us."[18]

—*Peter Senge*

SHOW ME ANYTHING on this planet, and I'll show you something that needs renovation, repair, refurbishment, tune-ups, and even upgrades on a regular basis. Even a rock wears down and eventually deteriorates to dust if left at the mercy of Mother Nature. In Disney's classic theatrical adaption of *The Lion King,* Rafiki calls this principle the "circle of life."

You know what I'm talking about here. You've seen it with your own eyes. If you want something to remain useful—a car, house, neighborhood, company, or even society itself—it needs to be regulaly repaired and rejuvenated.

Think about it. You've seen a farmer's field with one corner dedicated to old, dilapidated vehicles sitting on cinder blocks and rusting away in the dirt and weeds. The tires are long gone, the rubber rotted away to powder. Those cars, trucks, and tractors have been put out to pasture to die a slow, isolated, ugly death. Why? Simple: no one wanted to take the time and effort to give them a tune-up, splash on a new coat of paint, or repair worn-out parts. So there they sit. No one using them anymore. They will rust away in the spring rain, summer heat, and winter snow, season after season, year after year, until they eventually return to dust.

We went on lots of road trips when I was a kid, and I always sat backward in the rear- facing rumble seat of our station wagon. Perhaps I wanted to escape all my annoying sisters, or maybe they'd banished me and my smelly feet to the back for self-preservation, but from my vantage point, I always looked at where we had been, not where we were going. As we drove thousands of miles, hour after hour, to visit relatives through-out the West, I saw plenty of those old, private, pastoral junk-yards—and I always felt kind of sad. The deserted vehicles seemed to be looking at me with a pathetic, please-help-me look in their broken headlights, a reconciled grimace on their corroded grills.

In direct contrast to those junky old heaps, why do a few other cars age gracefully and turn into classics with renewed value and vitality? Why are some rare, timeless automobiles polished to a mirrorlike shine and shown off at weekend clas-sic-car expos, while most others end up in the farmer's field— or worse? The answer is obvious: someone renewed the classic to its former glory. Actually, the refurbished classic is usually *better* after restoration than it was when it was rolled off the showroom floor decades earlier.

Here's the bottom line whether you're talking cars or any-thing else. It's a law of nature. Everything on earth undergoes a natural process of decline and decay and needs tender, loving care on a consistent, ongoing basis. This is especially true of our own lives.

The Need for TLC

Humanity is constantly evolving, and progress is continually being made at an ever-increasing pace. This is truer right now than ever before. The technology of our world is accelerating at a logarithmic rate.

Let's consider cars again for a minute. Today, many of the replacement parts for old cars are better, stronger, and more resilient than the originals. Those who restore old cars polish every screw, bolt, and rivet with the utmost attention. There's the stark contrast: you have vehicles that rust away, abandoned in the farmer's field, and you have others that are constantly renewed and improved over time.

So what kind of car (or should I say car owner) are you?

The fact that you are reading this book tells me you are the type who will improve with age. You are the type who will maintain your value and vitality by continually learning, renewing, and growing. You are already part of the minority—a classic car that shines brightly as onlooker's gawk in awe at your timeless splendor, utility, and renewed value.

Learning is what you do when you are confident, active, curious, and want to understand the world around you. Learning can involve developing skills, acquiring knowledge, increasing awareness, solidifying core values, and amplifying your capacity to ponder and reflect on life itself. Real learning creates change, enlightenment, and a renewed inner peace balanced with self-esteem. Real learning generates a deep craving to learn and learn some more. It's a gift that keeps on giving, a brilliant form of TLC you give yourself.

In the stories that follow, you're going to learn about mental tune-ups and renewal. Just like the car abandoned in the corner of the farmer's pasture, you will figuratively die a slow, decaying death if your mind is not pushed, stretched, and pulled.

Stretching your mind involves setting some goals and being willing to be the best you can be. And one way you can do that is to watch others who have pushed the limits to become the best they could be. A perfect motivation is to watch the Olympics.

Learning from the Olympics

Have you ever stopped to notice that the Summer Olympics are always scheduled during the months leading up to our US presidential election? Maybe that's one reason I get so excited about the Olympics is that it gives me a break from the name-calling, mudslinging, prime-time candidate-degrading media circus the elections create.

Let's take the 2016 Summer Olympics as an example. Just think—if it hadn't been for the Olympics, I would have been dished up minute-by-minute, nauseating details about Donald Trump and Hillary Clinton. Instead, I was fixated on Katie Ledecky, Simone Biles, Michael Phelps, Ashton Eaton, Allyson Felix, Jordan Burroughs, and many more.

Most of my friends love watching the Olympics. I'm no different. I get so excited I can hardly stand it. I find myself checking the medal count at work on my smartphone, rewatching events on YouTube, and reading article after article about the previous day's activities.

I have my favorite sports, but during the Olympics I usually find myself watching kayaking, gymnastics, volleyball, swimming, and others I don't usually watch. Being an old wrestler, I love wrestling—yet during the Olympics, I watch dressage, weightlifting, and track and field. I have even been known to take in a bit of table tennis and archery.

Why do I find the Olympics so appealing? Why does my daily routine change for two weeks every four years? It can't be because I love all the sporting events. After all, I don't alter my life to watch the latest beach volleyball tournament or track-and-field meet when they're not part of the Olympics.

Here's what the Olympics bring to the table for me: I get to watch human beings accomplish feats and achieve goals that take years to master. I am enticed by the competition, patriotism, and drama of the stories behind the athletes. Like any athletic event, the unknown and the possibility of witnessing history is utterly captivating. Who does not marvel at an athlete who runs or swims faster than any other human in recorded history?

When I see those athletes standing on the podium, I cannot help but think of my own goals and aspirations in life. I see those athletes devote their all to accomplish a singular objective. I live vicariously through their unwavering dedication, resolve, vision, commitment, and, yes—blood, sweat, and tears—to capture excellence. For me, some of the most inspirational Olympic stories are not about the medals; they're about those who overcame Herculean odds to represent their individual countries.

Watching these athletes inspires me to be better—to be the best I can be. Seeing their incredible accomplishments tells me that hard work, perseverance, and relentless practice *does* pay off. It tells me you can push yourself harder and further than you ever thought possible. And it tells me that my dreams of learning can be realized if I am ready to put in the work.

I do a lot of activities in my daily life. I get up and exercise. I write. I make sales calls. I strive to improve myself and move forward. But can I do more? The Olympics give me the opportunity to admire the Olympians and their accomplishments. They motivate me to write down and more clearly articulate my goals and aspirations.

As you think about the Olympics in terms of your own life, ask yourself:

- What is your "event"?
- What dream or aspiration have you set as a goal?
- Are you really giving that dream your all?
- Are you truly committed, or are you just giving your dream lip service?
- What is inhibiting your ability to achieve your dream?

As you consider the phenomenal athletes who compete in the Olympics, think of your own personal goals. What do you want to master? In your journal or electronic notes, write down three things you can do to achieve those goals. Then get out your calendar and block out time to begin moving toward those goals no matter how scary that may feel. Be willing to do whatever it takes to learn the things that will bring you to the you, you really want to be.

Like Katie Ledecky or Michael Phelps, you will have to get in the water and start swimming if you want to become a swimmer; the same principle applies to whatever it is *you* want to do. You will have to get wet. You cannot just mentally sit on the side of the pool and go through the motions. You have to get in and work at it. You will have to engage your mind and seek the learning that will make the difference.

Diving into the Deep End

If you want to swim, then sooner or later you have to get in the water. So make it sooner! Decide now to jump in feet first—hell, dive in!—and get wet. Why hesitate? Shed those metaphorical floaties and jump into the deep end. It's not enough to sit on the steps in the shallow end. Take it from an old swim instructor—it doesn't work. Shallow water is too safe, and you'll never learn how to swim or see what your body is capable of if you always stay where your feet touch the bottom.

If the deep end is too intimidating, consult a friend who knows more than you. Hire a coach. Find out all you can. Talk with others who have been there and done that. But whatever you do, get in the pool and fight through those fears. Sitting in a comfy poolside lounge chair will accomplish nothing. Do whatever it takes to learn how to swim. Move from one side of the pool to the next. Before you know it, you will be doing multiple laps with ease.

In no time at all, you will gain strength, courage, and confidence. With each small achievement, you will move closer and closer to becoming the person you want to be. You'll become your very own version of those Olympic athletes. You'll develop the single-minded focus, determination, tenacity, commitment, hard work, and desire to achieve excellence. You will stand on your very own metaphorical podium, listening to your own national anthem.

Make no mistake: it will feel uncomfortable and maybe even strange at first. But what do you have to lose? In baseball, if you never swing at the ball for fear of missing, you will miss every time. The same can be said of anything in life. If you don't strive to become the best you possible, you will never become the best you possible. Years from now, you'll still be in the same spot you are right now, sitting on the side of the pool with floaties on each arm, watching others gracefully swim through life.

So think about those Olympic athletes. Watch some clips of their accomplishments. And the moment you feel that twinge of inspiration, go get your suit on and jump into the pool. Become the person you want to become. Set your own personal best records. Go faster and further than you ever thought possible. As the great Mahatma Gandhi said, "Live as if you were to die tomorrow. Learn as if you were to live forever."[19]

Olympic athletes are great examples of both physical prowess and mental agility. Consider this: when you work out, you are breaking the microscopic fibers of your muscles down so that they will grow back stronger and more capable. If you want to stay physically fit, you have to do that over and over. The same principle holds true with your mental muscle—your mind. Continually learning is like giving yourself a mental tune-up—and, in many cases, a mental upgrade. If you are not constantly learning, pushing, stretching, and exploring mentally, you will eventually go the way of the farmer's old Desoto. You will be driven out to the corner of the field where you will rust and die.

Learning is more important now than ever because of the rapid-fire changes in this world. Before I explain what I mean,

I'd like to share a little story about the birth of my oldest son and how he got his name—a story you will immediately appreciate as a vivid example of how the world has changed.

What's in a Name?

I recently called my eldest son to wish him a happy birthday. We laughed and laughed about the vivid memories I have of his birth, and as we did, I was instantly transported back to August 21, two decades earlier at a time when we were living in a small town in the Netherlands.

Please grab a seat in the back, buckle up, and take a spin with me as I demonstrate how radically things have changed (and how some things stubbornly haven't).

AJ was born in the small town of Leidschendam, Holland, during a time when our family lived in the nearby hamlet of Voorburg. He entered this world on the third floor of a small hospital in a room with a window overlooking a gorgeous green garden and large Dutch canal. It was a beautiful August day.

He was slow getting here once he decided he wanted out. He started out early—five and a half weeks, to be exact—with a rambunctious attitude of *I will do it my way*. But after that high-spirited start, he really dragged his heels, his mother laboring in great pain for several days to bring him into the world. I don't know how she had the strength; she endured it all like a champion.

In Holland—at least with AJ, that is—those who aided in delivering babies did not use forceps. Instead, they used a suction-cup device that attached to the crown of the head. I can still hear the small compressor engine extracting and pulling air as the doctor held the suction cup to his head.

I have a very weak stomach, and the sight of all that down there was making me weak in the knees. So I stayed up near his mother's head and tried to whisper encouraging words like "Don't forget to breathe," and "You got this." I think I annoyed and frustrated her more than anything.

I can't even begin to imagine how ready my wife was for it all to be over. It was obvious that AJ was close to making his appearance. Sure enough, once the suction cup was firmly attached to his head, the doctor started to pull on it and asked my wife to push.

The doctor's grasp was strong. The surgical tubing he was tugging on was getting stretched and very taut. This went on for a few minutes. I remember thinking, *Is this even healthy? Can this little guy withstand this powerful force?*

At that exact moment, the tension snapped, and the suction cup flipped back over the doctor's shoulders. Blood splattered all over the ceiling and the back wall. I swear I thought he had pulled our baby's head off. I almost fainted.

Lucky for all of us, it was nothing more than a false start.

The nurse couldn't help but notice that I wasn't doing very well. My jaw hung open, I was as white as a sheet, and panic washed over my face. She quickly reassured me all was okay. She was right, astonishingly enough. The doctor put the suction cup back on AJ's head, this time with a bit more force—and voilà! Out he popped.

There it was: August 21, 1996, at about 3:00 p.m., give or take a few minutes. The Dutch nurses and doctor nicknamed him King Arthur. After all, they knew he was going to be named Arthur. But more than that, the suction cup that had brought him flailing into the world had left his head with a prominent, red, crown-like mark encircling his head.

Even though he was more than five weeks early, he weighed almost seven pounds. Like most babies, he was an ugly little sucker. (Yes, moms, I just said that; stop rolling your eyes.) Like most parents, his mother and I were blind with pride and love. But make no mistake about it: he started this life as one unsightly creature.

In addition to the unfortunate features he shared with every other newborn on the planet, he had some extra liabilities. The suction cup had given him a serious conehead. A *serious* conehead. And that's not all. Because of the suction cup, he had a prominent red hickey covering his noggin, much like a bright-red beanie. Once the doctors assured me his deformed head would eventually assume a normal shape and the hickey would go away, I started to breathe again.

In the Netherlands, you must go to the *gemeente*—city hall—to officially give a child a name. And so it was that the day after AJ's birth, I eagerly walked into the *gemeente* in Voorburg holding the small slip of paper I needed to declare his name officially. Beaming with pride, I slid the paper with his proposed name—Arthur Ferrell Coombs IV—under the clerk's window.

And that's where it all started going downhill.

Because no sooner had I slid the paper under the window than a little old Dutch man speaking terrible English (very uncommon for the Dutch) approached the counter where I stood and informed me that it was against the law to give my child such a name. To bestow that name on him, I needed written permission from the Dutch royal family. It was the law. No exceptions.

At first I was shocked. What was he talking about? Then my shock turned to anger.

By then we had lived in Europe for almost seven years, and I thought I had seen just about everything. Well, it turns out I was wrong.

So you can understand what was going on here, a little history is in order. I need you to appreciate exactly how much has changed—and why it's important to learn about this stuff.

In the Middle Ages—before America was even a twinkle in anyone's eye—most places in the world followed the class system. That meant your station in life was determined by your lineage. If you were lucky enough to be born with a royal or noble bloodline, your future in life was almost guaranteed. If not, you were guaranteed to be a peasant. Nobody—and I do mean *nobody*—bucked the system and moved up. No matter what.

This was the way it was for hundreds, even thousands, of years. Tons of laws and rules were in place to make sure that those with wealth and power stayed wealthy and powerful and that those who were peasants, or commoners, stayed that way too.

Besides the obvious issue of income, there were some pretty brutal disadvantages for the commoners. Common people could not own weapons. Common people could not speak openly if they disagreed with the people in power. Common people could not worship how they wanted. Common people could not own land. You name it. In the United States today, we'd never put up with the things practiced back then. They would seem absurdly silly, unreasonable, and a violation of human dignity.

Before you start to get bored and drift off, here's where that class system collided with my son's name. Because there was a law *still on the books from the Middle Ages* that said no one could have a roman numeral in his name unless he had been born into a royal family—or given direct permission from a royal family—they wouldn't allow me to name him Arthur Ferrell Coombs IV.

Unbelievable. AJ was born in 1996, and that law was still being enforced.

So when I tried to name him in accordance with (and in honor of) our family lineage, the Dutch government would have nothing of it. They flat out denied my request. We weren't royalty, and I had no written permission. I tried to reason with them. I even pled with them. But my pleas fell on deaf ears.

After some frustrated sarcasm only an angry father can muster, I melodramatically told the Dutch authorities that my son may have been born in the Netherlands, but he was an American. I also told them that not having the freedom to choose whatever name you wanted was one of many reasons most Europeans left to come to America. It was why we Americans held so sacred our rights as individuals.

But that's not the end of it. As I was leaving, I told them I would not rest until I visited the American consulate in Amsterdam. And with as much Yankee smart-assery as I could muster, I said I would have my son's name officially registered as Arthur Ferrell Coombs IV, son of Arthur Ferrell Coombs III, son of the great Arthur Ferrell Coombs Jr., son of the noble Arthur Ferrell Coombs Sr. of Garland, Utah. Yes, I threw in the "great" and "noble" not just because they were great and noble but also because I wanted to rub it in that bureaucratic Dutchman's nose.

This one Dutch civil servant was aghast that someone other than "royal" family would take such action.

So AJ was named Arthur Ferrell Coombs IV—not because that was my name but because it was the name of his grandfather and great-grandfather. These men were honorable, honest, hardworking men who tried to do their best in life. I can assure you that his grandfather and great-grandfather made mistakes, just as I have. Yet without fail, they collected their thoughts and recommitted to doing the right thing. They learned everything they could about all kinds of things and made their lives better as a result.

Because they lived, my son lives. His grandfather and great-grandfather exist in his DNA and are part of him physically, mentally, emotionally, and spiritually. I see so much of them in AJ and what he does. The way he looks, the way he talks, the way he walks, the way he thinks, and all the other things he does are influenced by what he inherited from these great men.

As far as I know, the Coombs family line does not come from earthly royal lineage. AJ's great-grandfather was a hard-working businessman, a dry cleaner by trade. His grandfather was a teacher and entrepreneur. They both worked long, hard hours to provide for their loved ones. They both gave willingly to those in need.

I knew when my son was born that his name would be the single-most frequently heard words in his life. I hope that as he goes through life and hears his name, he will think of Grandpa and Great-Grandpa and learn from their wisdom, their mistakes, and their successes.

As his father, I hope he learns by studying what they did and how they responded to challenges, as well as from how I responded to challenges. Learning from family and those who raised you is the most important learning you can do in this life, and it will help you understand and help you handle any challenge that comes your way.

But, wait. Where did *AJ* come from? That's easy: his older sister, Kelly, came up with that nickname. She said he was kind of an Art Jr., and she liked the sound of AJ. So did the rest of us, and AJ stuck.

The day he was born was one of the best days of my life. I love him more than he knows—at least until he has a child of his own.

Then he'll know.

And that brings me back to the importance of learning because of the way things are changing. The world I grew up in and the world my older children grew up in are vastly different. Here's just one small example: if I wanted to chat with a friend after school, I had to use one of three phones in the house—knowing full well that my conversation was probably going to be heard by my parents or one of my snoopy sisters. Thank heaven for the fifteen-foot cord my parents bought that allowed me to take the receiver into the kitchen pantry for a bit of privacy. But I wasn't alone in my discomfort. I knew that the person on the other end of the line was in the same situation.

If I called a young lady, I was sure to get interrogated by my mom. And my female friend was sure to get peppered with questions from her parents as well. ("Who was that? And what did he want? Do I know his parents? Does he go to your school? How old is he? Is he a good young man?")

Now consider what things were like for my oldest son—you know, the one who almost didn't get the name we wanted to give him. He was able to instantly send a message—accompanied by pictures or a video clip—to *hundreds* of friends, male and female. And he could do it all with a high degree of confidence that the message he sent was completely private.

Now let's take it a step further and consider what the world is like for my two younger children. Seven to ten years later, they live in a world far different than the one their older siblings inhabited. My youngest daughter has made hundreds of friends in virtual equestrian worlds—young girls who love horses as much as she does—all over the globe. Saturdays, I will often find her video chatting with a group of friends from Sweden, the United States, Australia, and other countries as they ride their virtual mounts around in their simulated horse-friendly parks as if it were the most normal thing on the planet.

Yes, we live in an incredible time, when technological progress is so fast it is impossible to predict what things will look like in the long-term. As an entrepreneur, I am a believer and a participant in that progress. But I am also a parent, a writer, and a learner. I can see that something exceptional is happening to society.

Think about what society was like just a hundred years ago. For thousands of years, parents could expect their children and grandchildren to grow up in a world very much like their own. If I was a farmer, rancher, blacksmith, or fisherman, it was reasonable to assume my sons and their sons would be as well. As a parent, I could teach my children what my father taught me and what his father taught him. The very dirt I farmed was the same my grandfather had farmed—and the same my grandson would farm. The very property itself had been laid out and perfected by generations who'd worked the same piece of land. They knew without question that their posterity would be sipping ice tea and picnicking under the very tree planted sixty years earlier by a well-meaning great-grandpappy. I could plan for the future and impart sage wisdom to my children because I had truly been there and done that.

Not so today. Now we live in a world where long-term planning is anything more than two years. Society, humanity, and individuals are morphing into something our grandparents could not have possibly imagined, let alone planned for. Technology is the major facilitator of this change. Faster CPUs allow us to do ever more amazing tasks. We can move massive amounts of information in an instant at little to no cost. And the faster, cheaper, and more powerful technology gets, the faster it is renewed, reinvented, and upgraded.

With that technology-induced revolution has come a generation that is shortsighted. My parents wanted what was best for me and my siblings. Likewise, I want what's best for my children and their children. But there are large swaths of the future in which they will be living that I cannot possibly envision.

Could a Neanderthal ever have envisioned the life of a nomadic hunter-gatherer? Could the nomadic human appreciate or grasp the life of a farmer in the Middle Ages? Could a farmer living in the 1880s comprehend the life of a manufacturer in the 1930s? So it is with us, but instead of a change visibly happening every millennium, century, or even decade, the world we live in changes every year—and eventually more often than that. I believe the essence of laughing, learning, leading, and loving will be the same—but what we learn about, how we interact, and life itself will be radically different fifty years from now.

The world is shifting at such a fast pace that the trees I plant today will most likely not be enjoyed by my children and certainly not by my grandchildren. My kids will have moved. Their interests, work, and desires will not be the same as mine. My children's generation is working at jobs my parents could never have even imagined—jobs that can disappear or become obsolete overnight. This kind of change can and does create anxiety, uncertainty, and confusion.

Ready or not, the change is coming. If we are not learning, evolving, renewing, and upgrading our understanding of the world around us, especially in our vocational endeavors, we will be left behind. New technologies are reinventing the way we grind out a living and even the way we play—reinventing life as we knew it just a few years ago. In the job market, there is a premium for candidates who demonstrate their aptitude along with the impetus to learn and adapt. Those who are reluctant to learn technology are disadvantaged vocationally, financially, and even socially.

It's a fact that our age is one of constant change that necessitates almost equally constant learning. Those who do will thrive; those who don't will be left in the dust. The willingness to learn has *always* been important. I can help you understand precisely how critical it is by sharing a little story that involves a bunch of inexperienced Scouts, a tube tent, and a can of tuna. You'll get exactly what I mean.

Boy Scouts, a Bear, and a Backpack

As a youth, I loved hiking and camping in the High Sierra. The summer I was sixteen, having been a Scout for many years, I was asked to help the younger Scouts—about thirty of them—on their first fifty miler. We decided to start by hiking about thirteen miles out of Yosemite Valley to Merced Lake. It was a good hike climbing to Vernal and Nevada Falls and then continuing through Little Yosemite Valley and farther.

The night before we started, we drove in and camped in Yosemite Valley. I remember buddying up because, as was typical, we each had to share a tent with a friend. Whenever we camped, my buddy was almost always Dave Peachey.

We had many tent options, but that night we decided to use a tube tent and attach it to the tube tent of Mike Bacon and Ed Booth, two Scouts who were each about a year younger than we were. So we made one long tube tent we could enter from both ends. With our sleeping bags positioned in the middle and our heads facing each other, we could easily chat, play cards, and tell all those typical camping jokes.

Our Scoutmaster had warned us that there were black bears in the valley. Some of them had gotten quite aggressive with other campers, he said. I had spent a lot of time in the High Sierra backcountry, and I knew all too well how persistent and potentially aggressive bears could be when they wanted your food. I had learned it the hard way. More than once on overnight camping trips had I seen bears take food from other campers who had not properly stored it. And now I joined in by trying to teach the inexperienced Scouts that they needed to make sure all their food, toiletries, fishing bait, and other supplies were either in a "bear box" or properly hung from a tree, out of bear reach.

That was an especially important reminder for us because we hadn't even started the fifty miler; losing our food on the first night would have been problematic, to say the least. We older Scouts all made sure our backpacks were void of anything that would attract bears. Then we asked—and double asked—the younger Scouts to do the same. They assured us they had appropriately taken care of all their food. It was an important teaching moment, and we thought they were learning.

After dinner, we all hunkered down for a good night's rest before the first big leg of our weeklong adventure. I remember being partially asleep when I heard some rustling at the opposite end of the tent. I thought it must be Mike and Ed repositioning their sleeping bags or getting something out of their backpacks. But when I looked up, I was astonished to see a large, fat, black bear with a tan snout, upward of 350 pounds, quietly entering the tent on the opposite end about six feet from me.

I was stunned. I quickly and quietly woke Mike and Ed. I told them to quickly get out of their sleeping bags and exit the tent on our side. By this time, Dave was awake and was helping me get the two younger Scouts to safety.

Once out of the tent, I asked Mike and Ed if they had anything in their backpacks or sleeping bags that would attract a bear. They both assured me they were clean and could not imagine what the bear was looking for. I *knew* Dave and I were clean. We had spent way too many nights in bear country to make a foolish mistake like that.

We did the only thing we could do. We "got big," stood our ground, and scared the bear away by raising our arms and screaming, banging pots, and otherwise making enough noise to turn the heads on Mount Rushmore. The commotion woke just about everyone in camp. But it also achieved our objective as the bear quickly backed out of the tent and lumbered off into the woods.

We told everyone we had awakened about the bear. We forcefully drove home the point that bears can smell *anything* and that was why we had to be diligent with our food the entire trip. We couldn't afford *any* slipups. Then we all crawled back into our tents and sleeping bags. You can imagine the adrenaline coursing through our veins. After about twenty minutes of chatting, we finally started to doze off.

That's when I heard it.

It sounded like someone was walking around just outside our tent. I could hear twigs snapping and the soft rustling of pine needles and leaves. I thought it might be a Scoutmaster checking on the boys—or maybe a Scout going to the bathroom. But then the light of the moon cast a silhouette through the thin plastic used to form the tube tent.

It was no human.

It was a bear. A BIG BEAR.

It walked to the end of the tent, and when it poked his huge head inside, I could see it was the same bear. This time it was not so timid or cautious. It clearly had a mission—there was no doubt it was focused on something in our tent. I again woke the others, and we scrambled out the other end.

Once we were safely outside and the bear was all the way inside, we again started trying to scare the bear away. We shouted, banged pans, and blew horns. The bear did not flinch. All our noise and commotion did not faze it at all. It was intensely focused on something, and nothing was going to stop it.

The bear picked up Mike Bacon's fifty-five-pound pack and carried it away like it was weightless. I was struck by his strength, dexterity, and focus as it held Mike's pack in one paw so it would not drag in the dirt and scampered into the bushes.

The cardinal rule for dealing with bears in the backcountry is to let them have their quarry. Once a bear has what it wants—Mike's backpack in this case—you should never try to chase it down to get your stuff back. That will only incite the bear. It has what it wants, so leave it alone. And that's exactly what we did.

After the bear rumbled off into the woods, we all turned and looked at Mike, demanding to know what he had in his backpack. He stammered a bit and then said he had a can of tuna fish.

Okay, first of all, taking a *can* of anything on a fifty miler is dumb. Really dumb. You want your pack to be as light as possible, and hauling canned goods is not the way to do that. Not only that, but you have to haul the can back out when you are done eating what's inside.

Mike was embarrassed. He didn't think the bear would be able to smell through the can. And he had buried it in the deepest part of his backpack. His logic was sloppy, but he was new to backpacking. Finally, we all went back to sleep.

The next morning, I decided to look for Mike's backpack. To my surprise, I didn't have to go far. I found it in a small clearing of bushes about thirty yards from our campsite. Several things about it instantly struck me.

First, the pack was covered in a slobbery mess, but other than that, it was in very good condition. I had expected it to be torn to shreds.

Second, the pouch in which Mike had hidden the tuna fish can had been cut open along the zipper line. It looked like someone had used a razor blade to cut the pouch with great precision. It was a learning experience for me; I gained a new respect for a bear's claws.

Third, next to the pack sat the can of tuna fish—or what was left of it. It looked like it had been hit with a shotgun blast. From what we could guess, the bear must have held the can firmly with its hind legs and then used its two front paws to puncture the side and pull it wide open.

Finally, one of the saddest things I have ever seen was the can itself. It was licked clean. Not a hint of tuna fish remained—just slobbery blood. The bear must have cut its tongue on the jagged pieces of the can. But even with its tongue cut and bleeding, the bear had still licked the can completely clean.

The whole thing was a great lesson for the younger Scouts. We showed the boys how to very effectively hang a bear bag in the trees, and we had no more bear problems the rest of the week.

I have thought about this experience many times since.

When someone in our professional or personal life tries to teach us, to show us the way, there are several ways to react. First, we may simply not listen. Second, we may listen but choose to ignore the advice. Or third—and clearly the best option of all—we may listen and learn from others who have already taken the path.

Mike listened but chose to ignore our advice. His failure to take *all* the food out of his pack was born of ignorance. He honestly thought the bear would not be able to smell through the can. What a great life lesson. During entire rest of the fifty miler, Mike was more than willing to listen and follow the advice of the others who had been there and done that.

A humble, teachable attitude and the willingness to admit your ignorance or mistakes can help you avoid a lot of pain. But if you are one who knows it all, you will most certainly experience many large bears coming into your life's tent and walking off with your backpack before your journey has even begun.

Though few will openly admit it, some believe they know it all (just as Mike had felt). If you're one of them, news flash: you don't! Believing you have ALL the answers ironically limits your perspective on truth. Know-it-alls create division, isolating those who do not share their opinion. They may openly *talk* about connection, unity, and love, but their actions scream something entirely different. They are locked into a dangerous way of life that is full of shame, guilt, and foreboding heaviness (and sometimes a menacing bear).

They also tend to be isolated. They think they're the only ones who know how life should be lived. They start out by trying to convert those who have differing opinions. When that doesn't work, they apply judgment, shame, and guilt. When that doesn't make the others conform, they use humiliation, isolation, and control. Eventually, when that fails, they turn to hate, anger, and elimination.

Staying safely in your self-imposed prison of "I know all truth," living life as if you had blinders on, is a lonely existence. What is the fun of that? How will you grow and learn? You may as well have told God before coming to earth that you did not need a brain because you already knew all the answers. Why bother?

Then there are those who don't think they have all the answers but who refuse to make a move. Instead, they stay sheltered in their traditional way of thinking, trapped by the notion that what they know or believe is the ultimate truth. (Bears can't possibly smell tuna through a can.) They build walls around their ideas to ensure they stay securely inside their thoughts. Because they think *their* way of life is the only way to achieve happiness, they look at others with judgment and ridicule. They figure "the others" are wrong, misinformed, or just plain missing something. (Those guys can't make me take my tuna out of my backpack.) They instantly create an "us versus them," "me versus you," "this way or that way" ultimatum.

When you learn to entertain the opinions, ideas, and thoughts of others who do not totally think the way you think, you open yourself to new experiences, new skills, new knowledge, new friends, and new vistas. You open yourself to inclusion, not exclusion; acceptance, not rejection; tolerance, not bigotry; and love, not hate. As you learn new perspectives and expand your point of view, new, healthier pathways become visible and viable.

When you stop thinking you have all truth, you free up your ability to entertain new ideas, knowledge, and perspectives you never even thought possible. And just like our tuna-toting Scout learned, others have lots of really valuable information to share—some of which can even save your life.

The point of life is to leverage every experience—good or bad, simple or complex, painful or pleasurable—and to learn and grow from those experiences. You don't grow by being stuck in the same calculated beliefs and traditions.

Don't Be a Barnacle

Here's something you've probably never done: consider the life of a barnacle. Bet you didn't know that a barnacle is a member of the crab and lobster family. As a barnacle starts out in life, it has to decide which rock it's going to live on. Once that decision is made, the barnacle spends the rest of its life with its head affixed to a rock. The same rock. For its whole life.

Some of us are like barnacles. We attach our minds to a particular idea, tradition, or belief, and we stay stuck there—never moving, never exploring, never learning. Just like the barnacle, we are stuck in one location and one way of life. And just like the rusty car propped up on cinder blocks in the corner of the pasture, we slowly waste away our time on earth. We never get renewed, repaired, restored, or upgraded—and that means we lose our vitality and value in life.

I love this Arabic proverb that speaks to the value of knowledge:

> He who knows not and knows not he knows not, he is a fool—shun him;
>
> He who knows not and knows he knows not, he is simple—teach him;
>
> He who knows and knows not he knows, he is asleep—wake him;
>
> He who knows and knows he knows, he is wise—follow him![20]

Which of these describes you? Are you ever learning, seeking enlightenment from various sources, and testing and challenging conventional wisdom? Remember, if you're not learning, you are mentally atrophying. While the people around you are getting smarter, you're getting dumber. If you're not constantly learning, how in the world can you lead those in your office, home, or huddle? You can't! Learning is a prerequisite to leading and teaching. As President John F. Kennedy taught, "Leadership and learning are indispensable to each other."[21]

When you learn, you can start out with hitting the books—but before it's all over, you need to get personally involved in what you're learning. It was Benjamin Franklin who said, "Tell me, and I forget. Teach me, and I remember. Involve me, and I learn."[22]

One of the greatest things about learning is that it's always yours. Blues great B. B. King said, "The beautiful thing about learning is that nobody can take it away from you."[23] Those things that can't be taken away are among the great treasures in life.

Choosing Your Own Way

Recently I called a friend whose recorded voicemail message I love: "Make it a great day—it's your choice." That sounds so easy, and in many ways it is. *You* are the captain of your soul. *You* control your feelings, perceptions, and actions. *You* decide how you want your day to go. No one else on the planet can get you down, make you angry, or fuel your happiness.

That voicemail always reminds me of Viktor Frankl, one of the greatest men who ever lived. Frankl was born in Vienna, Austria, in 1905; he died in the same city ninety-two years later. It's what happened in between that makes him so amazing.

Frankl grew up in Vienna, the birthplace of modern psychiatry and home of renowned psychiatrists Sigmund Freud and Alfred Adler. A brilliant student, Frankl became interested in psychiatry. By the time he was sixteen, he had begun writing to Freud; he once sent Freud a short paper, which was published three years later.

He earned a medical degree from the University of Vienna in 1930 and was put in charge of a Vienna hospital ward that treated women who had attempted suicide. When Germany seized control of Austria eight years later, the Nazis made Frankl head of the Rothschild Hospital.

Frankl's history from there is staggering. He married a woman named Tilly Grosser. Nine months later, Frankl, his wife, and his parents were deported to Theresienstadt, near Prague, the first of four concentration camps he eventually came to live in. When his captors there noticed his skills in psychiatry, they ordered him to set up a mental health care unit to help newcomers overcome shock and grief. Later he set up a suicide watch in the camp.

Eventually, Frankl was sent to three more concentration camps: first, Auschwitz; second, a unit of Dachau where he spent five months as a slave laborer; and finally, another division of Dachau that was considered a "rest camp." He worked there as a physician until American soldiers liberated the camp on April 27, 1945. Despite incarceration in the four camps, Frankl survived the Holocaust. His family members were not as fortunate. His mother and brother died at Auschwitz. His wife was moved to Bergen-Belsen, where she died. The only other survivor of the Holocaust among Frankl's immediate family was his sister, Stella.

Now for the thing that makes Frankl remarkable: during his imprisonment in the camps, he keenly observed the people around him—captors and prisoners alike. He did everything he could to learn about the things in his environment, limited though it was. Then he secretly recorded his observations on scraps of paper, which he jealously guarded and managed to take with him to freedom.

Then he turned what he had learned into an opportunity to teach. One of two books he wrote from his notes on those scraps of paper was *Man's Search for Meaning*. The book not only chronicles his experiences as a concentration camp inmate but explains his extraordinary discovery: the importance of finding meaning in all forms of existence, even the most brutal ones—and thus finding a reason to continue living.

By the time of Frankl's death, *Man's Search for Meaning* had been reprinted seventy-three times and translated into twenty-four languages. It had sold more than nine million copies in the United States alone and has long been used as a standard text in high school and university courses in philosophy, psychology, and theology. Not too shabby. In a survey conducted by the Library of Congress and the Book of the Month Club, it was rated as one of the ten most influential books in America (*New York Times*, November 20, 1991).

And here's the profound truth we learn from Viktor Frankl. After watching thousands of people being subjected to the most inhumane treatment imaginable—and after suffering those indignities himself—he wrote, "Everything can be taken from a man but one thing; the last of the human freedoms—to choose one's attitude in any given set of circumstances, to choose one's own way."[24]

It is up to every one of us. *You* have the power to make it a great day—just as you have the power to make it a great life. Do not waste it. It is your choice.

Forgiving Your Way to Freedom

Forgiveness—the ability to let go of past hurts and wrongs—is an important part of making your life great.

As mentioned, I am a Civil War geek. I read about it. I watch PBS specials about it. When possible, I visit the battlefields and imagine the heroism and brutality of such a colossal conflict. Yep, I am that guy.

In the book *Lee: The Last Years*, Charles Flood tells the story of Robert E. Lee, the brilliant commander of the Confederate army. In that book is a story that speaks powerfully to us in our day.

After the Civil War, Lee visited a wealthy Kentucky woman who took him to the remains of a grand old tree in front of her mansion. There she bitterly cried that its limbs and trunk had been destroyed by federal artillery fire. She looked to Lee for a word condemning the North—or at least sympathizing with her loss.

After a brief silence, Lee said, "Cut it down, my dear Madam, and forget it."[25] In other words, it is better to forgive the injustices of the past than to let bitterness take root, poisoning the rest of your life. It's one of the most powerful lessons you can learn.

I find it fascinating that many today demonize Robert E. Lee, while others seem to embrace him as a cult leader of the alt-right. If you truly study Lee's life, you'll know that Lee would have been one of the first to condemn radical racial-hate groups of any kind. His statues can be a lightning rod for those who are reminded of the Civil War and why it was fought. I get it; I understand the hurt, pain, and frustration this remembrance might invoke. But I assure you Robert E. Lee would utterly condemn the hatred of those who still strive to carry, promote, and proudly wave the banner of white supremacy. He was a humble, gentle man I truly believe would have been reluctant to have statues in his honor anyway. He was about forgiving, forgetting, and moving on. He spent the latter part of his life pleading with many to forgive and forget. Lee would not approve of white supremacists wrapping themselves in Confederate flags and invoking his name to promote hatred and violence. This would be contradictory to Lee's most fundamental convictions.

And for those who look at Lee only as a military icon (positively or not), it would be wise to understand the significant enigma of Robert E. Lee: he was a supreme military leader who was humiliatingly defeated in a gruesome civil war and who then became one of the loudest, most visible, and ardent advocates of peace and unification.

But just like the wealthy Kentucky woman mentioned above, when wronged, we desperately want to have our pain and suffering understood and validated by those we believe should see it as we do. We become so fixated on our need to be justified that the lines are blurred, the truth is tainted, and reality is sensationalized. Some see the wisdom of General Lee as simple and obvious; others see it as unjust. After all, it's blissfully simple to talk about surrendering, letting go, moving on, and forgiving; but when the rubber hits the road and you're in the middle of the situation, it can be one of the hardest things you'll ever do.

When cornered near Appomattox, Virginia, out of options, and facing the utter destruction of the Confederate army, General Lee admitted this to his men: "There is nothing left for me to do but to go and see General Grant, and I would rather die a thousand deaths."[26]

Yes, surrendering, forgiving, and letting the anger go is hard—very hard. Yet there is an undeniable sweetness in laying down your sword and saying, "I will fight no more." Learning to master this skill is one of the true secrets of living a happy and fulfilled life . . . and I am still learning it.

It is impossible to interact with others without exercising some form of surrender or forgiveness. We cannot have any meaningful relationships without it. Whether the offense is minor or massive, the method and remedy are the same. And whether it is with my work colleagues, children, parents, siblings, or my ex-spouse, it seems I am consistently making apologies and seeking forgiveness. But I am also consistently learning.

It is the repeated cycle of offense, apology, and forgiveness that fuels and sustains any relationship. When forgiveness is genuine, real, and heartfelt, it's beautiful, freeing, and powerful. When this pattern breaks down, pride, ego, and selfishness poison the relationship; if not remedied, the relationship inevitably dies.

This is exactly the problem in many marriages, families, management teams, partnerships, athletic squads, and other types of relationships. Gandhi taught that if we practiced an eye for an eye and a tooth for a tooth, the whole world would be blind and toothless. Justice in and of itself simply cannot fuel and sustain meaningful human connections.

Mercy, compassion, and forgiveness are the true, driving force of any relationship. Surrendering, dropping all pretense, and truly letting go is hard but essential.

Many live their entire lives clinging desperately to the anger, bitterness, and pain inflicted upon them by someone else. Wives disparagingly vilify husbands, husbands blame wives, sisters demonize brothers, children malign parents, friends denigrate friends—and for what? Pride, ego, and vengeful gratification. These unhappy people selfishly strive to protect their reputation while trashing another's character.

I am reminded of a story by an author unknown to me. Many years ago in central Spain lived a father and son whose relationship became severely damaged. It became so rancorous the son decided to move out and never speak to his father again. After a few years, the father felt terrible about what had happened and decided to go out and look for his son. He searched and searched, but he couldn't find his son anywhere.

In a final, desperate attempt to find his son, make amends, and plead for forgiveness, the father took an ad out in the largest newspaper in Madrid. The ad read: "Dear Diego, please meet me in front of this newspaper office downtown at noon this Saturday. I am sorry. Please forgive me. I love you. Your father."

The next Saturday, there were more than four hundred young men named Diego waiting to see if their fathers had written the ad. Each one was looking for mercy, love, and acceptance from an estranged father.

So many in our society need to reach out and say "I'm sorry." On the other hand, there are countless individuals who need to metaphorically return home and lovingly embrace those who have wronged them. Forgiveness extends far past the grievance and rests on all involved.

Forgiving does not change what has been done, nor does it condone the offense. Forgiving does not mean you are saying "Everything is okay," "I don't care," or "What you did is no big deal." What it *does* mean is that you won't tuck the wrongdoer's offense away in the corners of your mind, waiting to use it as a weapon at a later date. It means you have learned how to let go and move on.

Of course, that's sometimes easier said than done when dealing with divorce. Often the most passionate and vexing relationship challenges are created when two individuals fall in and then out of love.

No one ever says "I do" with the remotest intention of someday saying "I don't." But sadly, divorce happens—it happens every day. People make bad decisions, trust is lost, love is twisted into hate, dreams are shattered, sides are chosen, and children become collateral damage. Words are exchanged, exes are vilified, lines are drawn, and denigrating variations of what happened are told and retold. The resulting deep hurt, resentment, and anger canker the soul.

While we outwardly tell ourselves and others that all is well or that we're doing great, our inner voice—the one we hear when we take an honest look in a mirror—whispers, "This is not entirely the truth."

I know firsthand how it feels. I know that when I harbor resentment and anger toward those I believe have wronged me, I am bound to them by an emotional link stronger and heavier than I can bear. The only way to break the link and to find freedom is to surrender—to ask for and to give forgiveness. And now I am trying to teach you what was so freeing for me to learn.

So choose to let go. Choose to surrender. Choose peace over anger. I am not faultless and realize that I carry much of the blame for the situations in my life, but I have learned all of those things through the painful lessons life has taught me. You have the opportunity to do the same, so choose wisely.

Such Deep Pain, Such Great Love

Several years ago, a dear friend gave me the book *Unbroken* by Laura Hillenbrand and encouraged me to read it. It chronicles the incredible life experiences of Louis "Louie" Zamperini. While I can't recount his entire story (it's truly amazing), I can give you my CliffsNotes version of the most poignant parts—

which, by the way, were woefully unexplored in the movie adaptation. Learning about Zamperini changed my life.

Zamperini was captured during World War II by the Japanese and spent twenty-eight horrific months in various Japanese prisoner-of-war camps. One of his oppressors was a man by the name of Mutsuhiro Watanabe, whom the POWs nicknamed "The Bird."

Watanabe was especially cruel to Zamperini. In prison, Zamperini was perilously near death as a result of weakness, starvation, and disease. Even while teetering on the brink of demise, Zamperini endured relentless beatings and other forms of brutality from the prison guards.

Watanabe often singled Zamperini out and seemed to find exhilaration in torturing him. He beat Zamperini with leather belts, batons, and with his fists and repeatedly vowed to kill him. The brutality is hard to read about and almost impossible to comprehend. Anyone who reads his story can imagine his pain and suffering and undoubtedly sympathize with his plight.

The POWs were liberated following the surrender of Japan in 1945, but long after the war ended, Zamperini found himself still imprisoned by hatred and a burning desire for revenge. His years of brutal torture had left him physically, emotionally, socially, and spiritually chained by his own cravings for vengeance. He often dreamed of his hands around Watanabe's throat, choking him to death; after each nightmare, he woke sweating and shaking in his own bed.

All he could think about was exacting revenge on the Japanese monster who had ruined his life. As he used alcohol to numb his torment, the nightmares and flashbacks continued.

Zamperini was now at the point of losing his wife and family. But he was saved from his self-destructive POW demons after hearing a sermon taught by an evangelical preacher.

With his new faith and outlook on life, Zamperini surrendered his hate and his longing for revenge on Watanabe. Freedom, joy, and peace now filled his heart, and there was no room for the rancorous odium that had consumed him.

Zamperini returned to Japan in 1950 to meet with the Japanese war criminals who were now themselves imprisoned. While there, he shook hands, embraced, and forgave many of his old camp guards. But one person was missing: Mutsuhiro Watanabe, The Bird. Watanabe had eluded capture and was never officially tried and punished for his war crimes.

After returning to the United States, Zamperini wrote a letter forgiving Watanabe of all the horrible things he had done and told him he felt no ill will toward him. The letter went unanswered. While in Japan carrying the 1998 Nagano Winter Olympics torch, Zamperini again tried to meet with Watanabe, who had by now reemerged but had never been asked to legally answer for his brutality during World War II.

The Bird declined.

I believe Louie Zamperini understood the concept of surrender with every fiber of his being. Even though Watanabe cowardly avoided any interaction with Zamperini, Louie himself had truly let go of the vengeful, angry, vindictive feelings debasing his soul.[27]

Next time you feel your anger rising in response to someone's hurtful actions, try to hear General Lee whispering in your ear, and lay your ego, pride, and anger down; it is time to surrender and forget it. It is better to forgive the injustices of the past than to allow them to remain and let bitterness take root and poison the rest of your life.

Sweet Surrender

I don't raise the flag of surrender often. But when I do, it is often with intense internal angst. Surrender is so, so hard! I, like Lee, would rather die a thousand deaths. It is in my DNA to fight for what I believe is just and fair in this life. Fighting for the truth, for love, for family, or whatever will make me happy and healthy—isn't that fair and just?

In every fight, there comes a point when I must ask at what cost I am continuing the battle. In some fights, I just need to throw my hands up and surrender.

In a way, surrender is the antithesis of control. Sometimes we become obsessed with a specific outcome, which often indicates that we want to change those who have hurt us. We want to take our pound of flesh and exact some pain from our offenders because that's what we believe they have done to us. I hope you will come to realize that your willingness to surrender achieves much more than your willingness to control.

We all have choices. Your surrender is not a sign of passively doing nothing. Instead, you're actively doing something from a place of peace. From a place of sweet surrender. From a place of strength.

Wherever you are in life—whether you are evading the black bears or waving the white flag of surrender—live your life with as much color and zest as you can muster. Stop thinking you have all the answers; you may just learn something new. Thinking you know it all restricts the acquisition of knowledge, connectedness, and abundance in life, while humbly admitting you have a lot to learn fosters growth, acceptance, and connection. When you think you have all the answers, it's time to crack open a new book, take a college course, or explore a new city, culture, or country.

No matter how many birthdays you've celebrated, never lose your zest for learning. We all know people who seem to start losing their lust for life as they age. For whatever reason, many stop pushing themselves. Maybe they think they know it all and, like the barnacle, are fixed to their ideas, refusing to look elsewhere for enlightenment. Perhaps they are just too tired to learn a new talent or start a new hobby. Maybe the aging brain is simply not as malleable, making things biologically more challenging, so they avoid things that seem hard and settle for what's easy. Perhaps life has thrown them a curveball they can't quite handle. Maybe some event caused massive injury to their self-confidence and they no longer believe they have the ability to achieve. And at the far end of the spectrum, some become so cynical and disheartened they simply give up, trudging through the rest of their lives as if half asleep.

Great industrialist Henry Ford said it all: "Anyone who stops learning is old, whether at twenty or eighty. Anyone who keeps learning stays young. The greatest thing in life is to keep your mind young."[28]

Lessons from the Other Side of Fifty

Take a minute to think about the important things you've learned in life. You probably know that living a productive, fulfilling life is not about the number of zeros in your bank account, the square feet of your home, the title on your business card, or the number of followers you have on social media. Living a genuinely peaceful life is not about achievement.

Living a rich, fulfilling life is about the process of personal improvement and rebirth. It is about living up to your real capacity, like those swimmers and runners in the Summer Olympics. It's about being the best you can be. The reality is that most people live boring, uninspired lives. Very few go to work because they want to; instead, they go because they have to or think they ought to. They wake to a complacency of their own making. They endure each day hoping that someday their ship will come in and that today will be that day. They buy lottery tickets, dreaming about winning and creating their own happiness. All the while they sit on the couch, tired and exhausted from the sheer boredom they experience daily.

Don't let that be you! Never stop learning. Never stop exploring and trying on new perspectives. Regardless of your age, revive your energy by learning something new. The thirties, forties, and fifties can be marvelous years of learning and laughing. Even those in their twilight years can renew and revitalize by actively seeking to expand their understanding of life.

Here are just a few things I have learned during my fifty-five-plus years. I hope they help you on your personal journey of learning. The most important life lessons for me are not about knowledge or skills. They are not about learning a new coding language, perfecting my management techniques, or improving my craftsmen skills. Those are all great things to have, but I don't believe they're the biggies that come as we age.

Instead, here are some of the things I consider the biggies:

I have learned to be easy on myself and not let my past enslave or define me.

I have learned to not worry about the things I cannot possibly control.

I have learned how to recognize my weaknesses and control their negative consequences.

I have learned to embrace and even encourage honest mistakes.

I have learned that failure is NOT failure—it is simply an opportunity to recalibrate my goals and strategies.

I have learned that happiness is a choice, and I have learned that anger, resentment, and jealousy can destroy happiness in a nanosecond.

I have learned that my reputation means little; what other people think of me is not nearly as important as what *I* think of me.

I have learned that laughter, learning, leading, and loving are the sturdy legs needed to support a table richly laden with joy and happiness.

I have learned that people and organizations who use shame, guilt, and judgment to create fear, intimidation, and control are not worth my time and energy.

I have learned that *I* create my environment. A Native American proverb states, "The wise Indian carries the weather with him." In other words, don't let the weather—or any other outside influence—determine, dictate, or influence your mood. *You,* not any external force, are the master of your happiness. That one lesson alone is critical to experiencing deep joy in this life.

I have learned that I sold myself short far too often as a youth. I know there will always be someone smarter, taller, stronger, faster, and more charismatic than I am—but I am far more capable than I realize.

I have learned that no matter how hard I try to please, plenty of people are not going to love me, and that's okay. It has nothing to do with my intrinsic value.

I have learned that I am blessed to have a handful of real friends and that I need to stay loyal to them, come hell or high water.

I have learned that the laughter of close friends is as valuable as pure gold.

I have learned that I can live either easy hard or hard easy and that it is my choice.

I have learned to live a life of peace and simplicity.

And I have learned there are only two things that are truly important to me—my time and my relationships. I protect closely what I do with my time and who I do it with.

Lessons like these don't come easy early in life. I've learned most of them in the ruthless school of living. As you travel your own life's journey, you will learn more about how to live a joyful life from the school of hard knocks than from any classroom you will ever attend. But in the process, make sure you listen to those around you who have already paid the price. What they teach can be invaluable.

The verdict regarding lifelong learning was deliberated and decided upon long ago. But the significant shift in how our world operates has made the importance of learning through-out your entire life far more important than it has ever been.

Having a positive attitude and a willingness for lifelong learning will define you as someone who laughs, leads, loves, and lives a full, rich life as you authentically connect with those around you.

Continual learning gives your mind the tune-up it needs and will ensure that you're not out decaying in the pasture, propped up on cinder blocks and wondering what the hell happened. A willingness to learn demonstrates that you're not the stubborn barnacle obstinately clinging to a belief or tradition that does not encourage out-of-the-box thinking, evolving, and learning.

So get off of the couch. Get out of the pasture. Decide to let go, and go explore a new rock.

§

CHAPTER 3

Leading: Unlocking People's Potential to Become Better

"If your actions inspire others to dream more, learn more, do more and become more, you are a leader."[29]

—*John Quincy Adams*

W E'VE NOW talked a little about laughing and learning. As you read the title of this chapter, you might well be asking, "How the hell does *leading* fit into this *L* concoction?"

Easy.

Here's a simple fact: you can't lead others unless you are living with, laughing with, learning with, and loving them. You may be able to *manage* them without those other four *L*'s, but you will never be able to *lead* them. And in the family, just as in any other enterprise on this earth, you never want to simply *manage*; you want to *lead*—because that's where you'll make the most powerful impact.

Let's take a look at how those other *L*'s are so connected to leading. And let's start with living—specifically, living large. You may wonder exactly what that means. You're undoubtedly familiar with it in some other form: *living life to the fullest, living a wholehearted life, living abundantly.* You can decide what you want to call it—but whatever that is, here's what it means: you throw yourself into life, taking advantage of the opportunities that present themselves and smiling whenever you get the chance. It doesn't necessarily mean living a life of financial and material abundance. It means being genuinely happy, truly fulfilled, and surrounded by people you love and who love you right back.

There's no room here in Living Large Land for standing on the sidelines. No holding back. It means you stop worrying about what happened in the past and start living in the present, with all it has to offer. It means you do what you can to bring your life into balance. It means you become more conscious and more alive and that you experience life the way it was meant to be experienced.

Living large does not mean living stupidly. So when you're looking at all the things you may consider doing, all the take-your-breath-away stuff you've never quite dared to do before, make sure you aim for balance. Balance doesn't mean playing it safe—it means picking yourself up when you fall, having an alternative plan, and taking risks now and then. It means getting in the game, not just watching from the sidelines.

The Barnyard Club

Whenever I think about living large, I remember a little treasure I found in the top of the barn that always makes me think about the importance of dads stepping up—and the importance of dads as leaders in general. And before you moms join a picket line and cast denigrating comments and malicious looks my way, please know that whatever I address to one demographic, I address to both. You'll see what I mean in a minute.

I don't know about you, but I have saved many of the little notes, drawings, birthday cards, and other artifacts my kids have given me throughout the years. I sometimes pull my box of cherished memories off the shelf and take a nostalgic stroll down Flashback Lane. It's like spending time with a long-lost friend.

While looking for something on the top shelves of my closet one day, I noticed a sheet of paper sitting on top of my treasure chest of little notes, letters, and keepsakes. That little sheet of paper made me chuckle when I first found it.

On Saturdays, I'm typically attacking some self-generated to-do list. Along with doing yard work, I putter in the garage, straighten the house, do laundry, and wash the car, among various other tasks. Occasionally, I petition, threaten, and bribe the kids to help me pull weeds (their least favorite chore). On many Saturday mornings during the spring, summer, and fall, you'll find me feeding the horses, mucking out their stalls, and doing general, all-around cleaning in the barn.

Early one fall morning several years ago, I was cleaning and winterizing the barn. Lady, our now-deceased thirty-three-year-old Arab—may she rest in peace—started banging against her stall, a clear indication she was old, bitchy, and hungry.

In order to feed Lady, I had to pull down a few bales of hay from the top of our mountain of alfalfa feed. So I climbed the stack of hay. Crouching so I wouldn't hit my head on the barn ceiling, I saw what I thought were dolls at the very top of the heap. That surprised me. It wasn't something I expected to find on top of our mountain of hay in the corner of the barn.

Puzzled, I decided to investigate. As I crawled over to the cramped corner, I found a few Barbie dolls, some towels, and a couple of zip-lock bags filled with old Oreos; the mice had probably been dining on them for the last several months.

I may not be Sherlock Holmes, but it wasn't too tough to figure out that my youngest daughter had been at the top of the barn playing with her friends and their dolls sometime that summer. Collecting the dolls, snacks, and accessories, I spied a piece of paper. When I checked it out, I realized it was a list of "club members."

It was the cutest thing ever. What made me smile was seeing *my* name on the list. Dad made the cut—and I didn't even know there was a cut to be made. Hell, I'd even made the list before the dogs and horses. That summer I was officially a member of "Mac's Barnyard Club."

I know that many families today do not have an *Ozzie and Harriet, Donna Reed Show,* or *Leave It to Beaver* story line and cast. Divorce is rampant; fathers and mothers die from cancer or car accidents; some parents are deployed long-term to all corners of the earth for military or vocational reasons. We do not live in a society where June Cleaver meets Ward Cleaver at the door each evening at five with a kiss and a plate of freshly baked bread.

I am not a perfect single dad. I fall woefully short in so many things I do and don't do. But I have never missed a mandatory school event, and I made the cut in my daughter's barnyard club. When I start feeling anxious that I am not doing enough as a father, I look at Mac's club list and smile. It says, *Art, you are okay. Keep doing what you are doing. You made the cut. Now check your schedule and make sure you are in town for "Donuts with Dad" this fall.*

The most important job for all dads and all moms is to step up and live large with the people who are most important in your life. Be a leader in the very best sense of the word. Do it for you, but even better, do it for them.

Using Humor as a Tool

Now let's take a look at laughing as it relates to leadership.

Humor can either accelerate or undermine leadership—and that's true in any setting, from the corporate boardroom to the family room. It's all about how you *use* the humor. If you're trying to be funny and to unite people, humor is a great tool.

More than five decades of research from all the biggest think tanks, consulting firms, and prestigious universities proves that humor—when used authentically, skillfully, and kindly—unites, motivates, and focuses teams as they strive to accomplish goals. When stress mounts and emotions start to get the best of everyone, humor can be used to defuse, readjust, and calm tensions. Let me give you a real-life example.

One summer I was on a Delta flight from Orlando, Florida, to Salt Lake City. Based on all the hats with ears and the more-than-occasional Disney-themed clothing, the plane seemed to be full of happy families returning from the Walt Disney resorts in the Orlando area. As we flew over the Rocky Mountains, the pilot informed us that there were heavy winds and potential severe turbulence ahead as we approached the airport. He told everyone, even the flight attendants, to sit down and buckle their seat belts. He gave the warning a second time, and everyone strapped in for an exciting, bumpy approach.

He was right in his prediction. As we approached the Wasatch Front of the Rocky Mountains, the plane started to violently shake, drop, and tilt from side to side. After several powerful jerks and jolts, everyone on the plane realized that this was going to be a tense landing.

Those of us on the plane who had millions of miles under our belts could tell this was no ordinary turbulence. No, this was something far more severe. The cabin became completely silent, as if we needed to let the pilot concentrate on his task. I looked around and noticed that some were calling on a higher power to aid our plight. It was painfully obvious from the tense faces and white knuckles I could see that the anxiety level in the plane was off-the-charts high.

For what seemed like several minutes, the plane continued to lurch ferociously up and down and violently list from side to side. The strength, intensity, and menacing rumble of the storm's fury was alarming; it felt like our massive airliner was being tossed around like a whiffle ball. Those sitting by the windows could *see* the wings shaking violently in the high winds.

No one made a sound as we approached the airport. The pilot had the plane at an acute angle as we descended toward the runway. We seemed to be flying sideways. Then, at the last minute, the pilot straightened the plane. Suddenly it seemed to slam into the ground with a massive thud. We bounced around for a few uncomfortable moments as we rumbled down the landing strip. As the airplane started to slow, you could tell everyone on board was more than a little unnerved. Finally, the plane shuddered to a stop.

As we sat there in speechless silence, processing what had just happened, the pilot's voice crackled over the sound system: "And you thought the rides at Disney World were exciting.

Folks, welcome to Salt Lake City." We could easily hear the grin in his words.

All the passengers looked at each other for a split second and then exploded with laughter, cheering, and applauding. He had managed to change the entire mood of that airplane in mere seconds with one simple, lighthearted, funny comment. We instantly transitioned from massive anxiety, stress, and fear to shared laughter, smiles, and a feeling of togetherness.

Excellent leaders balance the intuitive, emotional, gut-feeling side with a rational, facts-driven intelligence side. They have deep self-awareness and an extraordinary ability to empathize. The ability to use humor, especially while under stress, is a sign of a leader's high emotional intelligence. These leadership traits are key in the effective use of humor. They are the difference between the perfectly timed one-liner and a sarcastic, cutting gibe that falls flat or stings.

When a leader can express appropriate humor in a stressful situation, it communicates to others a calm confidence that all is well. This quick-witted, cool composure is what separates great leaders from those who merely pretend to be leaders. And according to my kids, "Everyone can spot, and nobody likes, a poser or a wannabe. It just ain't cool."

Joe Cool

When I think of leaders and cool, I think of Joe Montana—a guy nicknamed "Joe Cool." Montana emerged in the 1980s as the perfect model of the NFL quarterback. His composed play in high-pressure situations demoralized opponents while simultaneously thrilling San Francisco 49er fans.

One classic illustration of his coolness under pressure happened during the 1982 Super Bowl, which pitted the 49ers against the Cincinnati Bengals. The 49ers trailed sixteen to thirteen with just three minutes and twenty seconds left in the game and had the ball on their own eight-yard line. They had to go ninety-two yards in just a few minutes. That would be hard enough under *any* condition, but think of how freakishly brutal it must have seemed under the intense pressure of the Super Bowl.

In his own words, Montana remembered that "some of the guys seemed more than normally tense, especially Harris Barton, a great offensive tackle who has a tendency to get nervous."[30] As usual, Montana was focusing on the entire situation—how far they had to go, how much time remained, and the plays that had been called.

As they gathered in a huddle, Montana spotted the comedic actor John Candy in the stands. "Look," he said to his teammates, pointing into the stands, "isn't that John Candy?" It was definitely *not* what his teammates expected to hear from their leader, there in the huddle with a few short minutes on the clock and the Super Bowl hanging in the balance. But it was that quick, casual comment that broke the tension and helped everyone in the huddle to focus. "Everybody kind of smiled," remembered Montana, "and even Harris relaxed. Then we all concentrated on the job we had to do."[31]

And what a job they did under his leadership. The 49ers did indeed march the ball ninety-two yards. With just seconds left in the game, they scored a touchdown and went on to win twenty-six to twenty-one. That day, Joe Montana was awarded his first of what would become three Super Bowl MVP trophies.

It was Grenville Kleiser who stated, "Good humor is a tonic for mind and body. It is the best antidote for anxiety and depression. It is a business asset. It attracts and keeps friends. It lightens human burdens. It is the direct route to serenity and contentment."[32]

Laugh at Yourself

Another clear sign of the connection between laughter and leadership is the ability to use humor in a self-deprecating manner. One of my favorite and most admired leaders, as you recall, is Abraham Lincoln. In a political world where all too often we hear nominees, the press, and society at large bombastically attack, ruthlessly belittle, and tear each other down in a feeble attempt to make themselves look good, we seldom see politicians with the wit, humility, and humor Lincoln displayed. He was a master of easing tension with a quick joke or story. It didn't matter if he was engaged with the press, entertaining his cabinet members in the Oval Office, or inspecting the troops on the front lines, he could teach a moral more prophetically and more efficiently with a humorous story than he could using all the evidence, opinions, and political pomp-assery under the sun.

Lincoln had two prominent physical characteristics that often made him the brunt of jokes among friends and enemies alike. First, he was six feet, four inches tall; back in his day, that was unusually tall. Not only that, but he was *extremely* skinny; the combination made him appear lanky and awkward. This garnered him the nicknames "Scarecrow" and "String Bean." His second prominent feature was a homely face (likely caused by Marfan syndrome), which people said could frighten children and even horses. His face earned him another mean-spirited nickname: "Gorilla." Despite it all, Lincoln was bulletproof. He told jokes about himself that were better and funnier than the ones told by his enemies.

Once, while speaking at a conference of newspaper editors in Bloomington, Indiana, he expressed that he felt uncomfortable there because of his lack of editorial credentials. He said he wondered whether he should have come at all. "I feel like I once did when I met a woman riding on horseback in the woods," he related. "As I stopped to let her pass, she also stopped, and looking at me intently, and said, 'I do believe you are the ugliest man I ever saw.' Said I, 'Madam, you are probably right, but I can't help it!' 'No,' said she, 'you can't help it, but you might stay at home!'"[33]

Lincoln's ability to not take himself too seriously was one of his most endearing traits. His self-effacing, humble, calm demeanor soothed many an anxious individual while dealing with the nation's most serious test—the Civil War. On one occasion, Lincoln was accused of being hypocritical, or two-faced. In reply, he said, "If I had two faces, why would I be wearing this one?"

Lincoln knew that this humorous, self-deprecating style would sooth the antagonist, stifle criticism, ease stress, improve morale, and help communicate difficult messages. He did not become offended and go on the attack when others made fun of him or put him down. Instead, Lincoln used his self-deprecating humor to bring friends and enemies alike into his circle—to help them understand his feelings and teach lessons the common man could relate to. He used humor to connect and lead, demonstrating a keen sense of self and a high emotional intelligence. When he laughed at himself, everyone—even his enemies—laughed *with* him, not *at* him.

If you cannot laugh at your shortcomings, mistakes, and weaknesses, you will never be a real leader. Leadership is explicitly connected to and demonstrated through kind, well-timed, genuine humor. Leaders have a self-awareness that exudes a calm, happy demeanor others innately want to follow.

Humor focuses our minds, fortifies our relationships, and helps us manage stressful situations. It doesn't matter if you are trying to land a plane in severe weather, attempting to deflect a nasty insult, or trying to cope with daily life; humor is a positive, calming leadership tool when used appropriately. If you can laugh at it, you can learn from it. If you can learn from it, you can teach it. If you can teach it, you can lead it. So let's all lighten up—smile, giggle, and laugh. It's good for you and everyone around you.

There *is* a caveat to humor: you should *never* use humor at someone else's expense. If your humor makes fun of someone else in any way, you have gone out of bounds. You will alienate people and undermine your leadership—and trying to recover with an impetuous "You know I'm kidding" simply won't fly. There is no excuse for a leader of any kind to laugh at someone. Putting others down is rude and hurtful. People remember hurtful comments for years, and such humor can bruise, break, or completely destroy relationships. Laughing at the weaknesses or ignorance of others is arrogant and shows the empty, egotistical character you are masking.

A story I first heard my father tell when I was a very small boy taught me a tremendous lesson about laughing at another's expense. I heard him tell it on a number of different occasions, and I will now tell it from my own perspective and memory. My father affirmed that it's a true story, but he heard it from another storyteller sometime around 1950; he didn't know the original author, and neither do I. Regardless of its origin, it demonstrates the danger in using humor at someone else's expense more powerfully than any story I've ever heard.

Gabby

In 1947, Alan was a seventeen-year-old living in Salt Lake City, Utah. In between his sporting activities and during the summers, Alan and his friends found work in local factories near his home to earn extra money. That year, World War II was still winding down, but many of the factories remained very much alive, crawling with female and teenage workers.

While tensions were easing and the United States was eagerly getting back to building a country and away from fighting a war, factories were shifting from the manufacture of military to civilian products. That summer, Alan found work in a local factory—a brewery—with several of his friends.

At that time, manufacturers were largely driven by manpower, and the companies worked their employees with few breaks. Alan and his friends sometimes burnt off pent-up teenage tension by what they thought was innocent horseplay—teasing, wrestling with, and playing practical jokes on each other.

One of the leaders at the factory was Jack, a young man in his early twenties. He was large, strong, and witty—the jokester who constantly played pranks on others. Then there was Billy. A follower, he always went along with Jack. There were others, of course, but Jack was always the lead, and Billy his right-hand man. Alan was never sure why he was accepted by Jack, Billy, and others because they were three or four years older than he—but he loved being accepted and part of the "in" crowd.

One coworker bore more than his share of Jack's practical joking. He was just a little different. He was considerably older than the rest of the young men who worked in the plant. He dressed oddly, often wearing pants with patches and shirts that had clearly been purchased at the thrift store. He was thin and gaunt, as if he were constantly ill, and he had more than a few teeth missing. He was slow of speech and uncoordinated. He was a loner in a harmless way. Jack nicknamed him Gabby.

Why Gabby? It was just one of many jokes they played on him. He didn't speak much and stayed to himself. *Gabby* was the title they mockingly gave him due to his shy, quiet, aloof nature.

As summer turned to fall, the factory began to slow its production. Many of the younger employees worked shorter evening and weekend shifts. As the work demand eased up, Jack's boredom and practical joking picked up.

Gabby would often find a live frog in his lunch pail or a dead rodent in his hat. But he always took the pranks in stride and quietly went about his business.

One day, Jack, Billy, and a few others took a few days off to go hunting. As they were planning their hunt and before they left, they assured Alan and the others that if they got anything, they would bring everyone at the factory a good piece of meat from the kill. So those at the factory were all genuinely excited when the hunters returned and they learned that Jack had gotten a nice, big bull elk.

Before Jack came back to work, Billy started bragging to some of the guys about the hunt and their heroics. Billy never could keep anything to himself, and it leaked out that Jack had a fantastic practical joke to play on Gabby. Jack had butchered the elk and had made a nice package for everyone at the plant. However, just for laughs he'd saved the ears, tail, and hoofs. He and Billy thought it would be hilarious to give them to Gabby and have him unwrap them in front of everyone.

The next Saturday quickly arrived, and the victorious hunters came to work. At a lunch break, Jack began distributing the packages. They all were carefully wrapped in white butcher paper. Everyone opened their packages just enough to see they'd gotten a nice piece of meat, then thanked Jack and the other hunters for their gift. Jack saved the biggest package of all for last. It was for Gabby.

Alan stood off to the side, feeling somewhat uncomfortable as Billy was all but bursting with excitement and Jack was looking smug, straight-faced, and theatrical. Like always, Gabby was sitting off by himself in the back, watching. Jack then raised the largest package of all and said with a grin, "Gabby, this one is for you." Gabby came up front and held the large wrapped gift in his hands. Everyone sat and waited.

Gabby was never one to say much. In fact, one might never even know he was around; he was one of those people who said nothing and shied away from being the center of attention. The entire time Gabby had worked at the factory, he had said less than a handful of words to anyone. So everyone was spellbound by what Gabby did next.

Gabby took the package firmly in his grip, feeling its weight and size, then slowly looked up at everyone assembled around the large table. Gabby smiled broadly at Jack, and it was then that Alan noticed Gabby's eyes were red and moist. His prominent Adam's apple began to bob up and down, and his lips quivered for a moment before he got control of himself.

Then Gabby began to talk.

"I know I haven't seemed too chummy with you guys, but I never meant to be rude. You see, I've got nine kids at home and a wife who is very sick—bedridden for many years now. Doc says she ain't ever going to get better. And sometimes when she is real bad off, I have to sit up all night to take care of her. And most of my pay goes to doctors and medicine. The kids do all they can to help out, but at times it's been hard to keep food in their mouths.

"Maybe you think it's odd that I go off by myself to eat lunch. Well, I guess I've been a little ashamed, because I don't always have anything between the bread in my sandwich. Or like today, maybe there's only a raw potato in my lunch pail.

"But I want you to know that this meat means a lot to me—maybe more than to anybody here. Because tonight, my kids—" Gabby wiped the moisture from his eyes with the back of his hand. "Tonight my kids will have a meal." He then began to tug at the tape sealing the package.

Alan was sickened by what was playing out. He had to do something. Being fast, athletic, and one of the closest to where Gabby was standing, Alan dove for the package to try to grab it. He nearly cracked heads with a few others who had the same idea.

But everyone was too late. Gabby had broken open the neatly taped, tight, white butcher paper and was already examining its contents. He closely scrutinized each hoof, ear, and then the tail. You could hear a pin drop when he slowly held up an ear and it wiggled limply.

It should have been so funny. But nobody laughed. Nobody at all.

The hardest part of all was when Gabby looked up at everyone and awkwardly tried to smile.

I never in my life remember my father playing a practical joke on anyone. It was not in his nature to laugh at the expense of others. The story of Gabby has strongly influenced me and impacted the way I have tried to raise my children. As a young man, I admit I was a prankster—and I look back on some of my teenage mischief with regret. Ever since Kelly, AJ, Kai, and Mac were very small, I pleaded with them to be the natural leaders they intrinsically are. I have taught them that real leaders stand up and protect those who cannot protect themselves. While I was a bit of a hellion, I hope and pray that Kelly, AJ, Kai, and Mac will be strong enough to speak up for others, even when it's not popular. When it comes to playing practical jokes on others, I pray my children will follow their grandfather's amazing example more than their father's.

I hope you now understand the vital link between laughing and leading. Now let's look at how learning and leading are connected.

Leaders Must Be Learners

We've already talked about how the world as we know it is evolving at such a rapid pace—and if you aren't learning, you're falling behind. Learning is one of the most powerful and effective skills a leader can develop and encourage—not only in themselves but in those they lead. In fact, many argue that the ability to learn may be the most valuable competency in leadership.

New global challenges will require new leaders with newly minted skills, whether at work or home. And if you hope to rise to this task, you will need to constantly question the traditional way of doing things. You cannot afford to stop learning. Ever.

What we thought was good or even great a decade ago is now—or soon will be—passé and old school. Leadership attributes and abilities that worked in the steady, predictable environments of the past will seem absurd in our new, fast-paced world, where we can hardly *see* and delineate future problems, much less *solve* them.

As a leader, it's essential you have the "I want to learn" gene in your DNA. This attitude implies that you don't have all the answers but are eager to find them out—and you openly confess this reality to your team.

If you're anything like me, you've had plenty of experiences where you realized you *didn't* have all the answers. One of the most memorable for me was the time I competed in the Olympics.

Yes, you read that right—I competed in the Olympics. Well, sort of.

Before you run to the internet and start searching for my name on the rosters, I should probably explain.

The Table-Tennis Thumping

During part of my youth, I was an Explorer Scout. Explorers were the young teenagers fourteen to eighteen who wanted to continue enjoying the benefits of the Boy Scouts and the Girl Scouts as they grew older. The focus of Explorers was to develop some career skills that would help prepare them for adulthood.

And believe it or not, they hosted their own Olympics. Young men and women came from all over the globe to represent their individual geographical areas and participate in twenty-nine different sports. Most of those sports were the same ones that were part of the real Olympics.

That's where I came in. In 1978, I was asked to represent my region in the National Explorer Olympics in Fort Collins, Colorado, in wrestling.

As we arrived, we were taken to the Olympic Village—just like at the real Olympics, only ours was on the Colorado State University campus. Before anything too serious happened, we settled into our dorms, got a feel for the campus, and checked out the week's schedule. Then we went to the opening ceremony.

I remember being a bit stunned by the sheer size and scope of the opening ceremony. For some reason, I had expected a small, poorly organized sporting event with a few hundred participants. Boy, was I wrong. Thousands of athletes from all over the country swarmed into the opening ceremonies, many of them international athletes having traveled from other countries.

After the opening ceremonies, the adrenaline started pumping, and we started mentally preparing for our respective events. Wrestling was to start on Thursday, so I looked forward to being a spectator for the first few days of the Olympics.

That first evening, our adult leader, Roy Hall, came to our dorm and pulled our group aside. He had learned that many of the events were not completely full—including archery, a few track-and-field events, team handball, water polo, judo, and others. He told us if we were interested and these events didn't conflict with our primary events, we could enroll and participate.

The one that captured my attention was table tennis.

When I found out that none of the table-tennis events conflicted with my wrestling matches, I thought, *I can do that. What the heck! It should be fun, and who knows? I may even medal.* I chuckled at the thought of being both a wrestler and ping-pong player in the Olympics. What a sporting oxymoron.

Wow, did I have a lot to learn.

Oh, I thought I knew a lot about table tennis. After all, I was not without experience. You see, we had a ping-pong table in our basement. My dad and I played once or twice a month. My father was very good—and he was the best trash talker I ever knew. He always held back, kept the score close, and then almost always won while verbally poking fun at his opponent with a gentle, taunting smile.

The oft-repeated scenario went something like this: As he was hunched over, about to serve, he'd say, "Art, are you ready?"

"Yes, Dad—I'm ready."

Then he'd stand up straight and ask again, "No, really. Are you ready?"

"Yeeesss, Dad; I am ready."

"I don't think you're ready."

"Dad, I swear I'm ready!"

With that, he'd hit a wicked spinning serve I almost always slammed into the net or off the end of the table. With a cheeky grin, he'd fetched the white plastic ball and said with the kindest smile you have ever seen, "Let's try that again . . . or perhaps you need to warm up a bit more? We don't have to count that last one if you don't want to."

I would shake my head, chuckle, roll my eyes, and say with renewed determination, "No, let's count it, and let's play."

For the rest of the game, he would get in my head with his smack talk and frustrate me while simultaneously making me laugh. As I got older, our scores grew closer and closer. He could still beat me most of the time, but I had my moments.

Back to the dorms in Fort Collins. After our short meeting with Roy Hall and the rest of the athletes in my group, I signed up to represent our area in table tennis. I didn't bring a paddle, of course, but I was sure someone there would lend me one.

The table-tennis event was to start on Monday—the very next day. I went to a large gymnasium on campus where there were eight or ten brand-new, clean, green ping-pong tables set up in a neat row down the middle of the floor. Bleachers rimmed the gym on a second level, giving spectators a comfortable view of the games being played below. A large bracket was pinned to a corkboard near the main officiating area; it looked like about thirty-two athletes were signed up.

I scanned the bracket for my name. I was to be on table three at 10:00 a.m. I had plenty of time to poke around and beg some stranger to lend me a paddle. In no time at all, I found myself standing at one end of table three in my jeans and polo shirt; a man sat near the side of the table to act as umpire and scorekeeper. I did some light stretching and bounced the ball on my paddle as I waited for my first opponent. (As if I were going to face many opponents. Little did I know.)

The next thing I saw was the double doors on the far end of the gymnasium swing wide. The light from outside shined through brightly. Two Asian men entered in a slow, controlled jog. Following close behind was a small, slender Asian teen in sweats. Completing the entourage was another pair of older Asian men toting what looked like gym bags. They swept into the gym as if gearing up for a prime-time boxing match. Not only were they all dressed alike, but they all also looked at me with a menacing scowl—in unison. They made their way right up to my table and stopped.

I was speechless.

The young man in the middle looked at me and bowed in my direction. He then faced the scorekeeper and bowed to him as well. He looked *so young*—I figured he was twelve or thirteen, but no older. The other four took a seat on a bench reserved for coaches. Holy Hanna! This kid had *four* ping-pong coaches? I was still trying to process what this all meant when the young man took off his sweats and revealed an extremely anemic look-ing frame clothed in a bright-red uniform embroidered with ping-pong paddles and what looked like Chinese characters.

My opponent looked at me, looked back at his ping-pong entourage, and then back at me again. His brow furrowed; his eyes squinted. He spun back around, and one of the coaches held one of the gym bags open. He started rummaging through the contents of the bag.

Double Holy Hanna! There must have been twenty ping-pong paddles in that bag. He picked one up, ran his finger over the rim, and looked back at me. I must have looked like a fish out of water. There I was in my stocky wrestling physique, jeans, and polo shirt, with an old, tattered, borrowed paddle and not a coach in sight. And even though I didn't realize it then, I had *so much* to learn about table tennis.

With his chosen paddle in hand, my opponent made his way to the table, and we began to volley the little white ball back and forth to warm up. After a few minutes, we each made a few practice serves.

Before we had even played a single point, I could tell I was in *way* over my head. I was not even *close* to this kid's league—and that was a massive understatement.

The umpire flipped a coin, and my opponent won the toss. He opted to have me serve, and I got to choose the side of the table on which I wanted to play first (like that mattered).

Game on. I tossed the ball in the air and tried my best to emulate my father's spinning serves. But with each serve, my young opponent hit what seemed like a slam to me, and I stood there as if my feet were submerged in quicksand, watching a white projectile whiz past my head. After five quick serves, the score was Young Asian Kid, 5–Art, 0.

Now it was his time to serve. He held his paddle with what looked like a distorted, disfigured grip in some freaky, up-side-down position. He got low and tossed the ball a few inches in the air. With a slight grunt, he ripped a spinning serve that caused the ball to bounce and swerve in a completely unpredictable pattern. The same thing happened again and again.

And just like that, the score was 10 to 0.

I think the entire match lasted a dizzying fifteen minutes—maybe even less. By the time it was over, it was three games to zero. And I did not score a single point. You heard me—not one single point. I truly tried, but I got a ping-pong ass kicking unparalleled in the history of the sport. After the match, he bowed politely and shook my hand. I have to laugh as I reflect on what must have been going through his head.

I just stood there with a stunned expression on my face. Finally, one of the Asian coaches came up to me and asked in a hushed, respectful tone and with careful broken English, "You come here for ping-pong?"

My chance to redeem myself! "No, I am here for wrestling. My leader asked me just last night to sign up for table tennis."

His eyes got wide, and he nodded his head as if the light had just gone on. Then he said, "Ohhh, I see. I think it best you stay with wrestling."

I smiled. "Yes, I think that is good advice."

And just like that, my table-tennis-playing endeavors were restricted to pickup games with friends and my father in our basement.

My stint at the Olympics was certainly memorable. I learned that if you want to do something really well and compete on a high level, you cannot go about it with a mediocre or laissez-faire effort. When you're talking about an important issue, a "good" effort usually yields ordinary results. And, as was illustrated by my ping-pong experience, an average effort usually delivers dismal results.

Had I known I was going to be playing table tennis at the Olympics with a ping-pong prodigy, I would have prepared a bit more. Even then, practicing with my teasing father ten times as much would not have changed the outcome. It was evident this young man had spent serious time with serious coaches to perfect his craft. He was not just good—he was the epitome of ping-pong excellence. He was a prime example of continual learning.

When you are striving for excellence, you need to focus, commit, and prepare as if your very life is at risk. Think about that. Do you want to succeed that badly? If you do, you will invest unbelievable time, energy, and focus in preparing yourself. You will learn everything there is to learn about the endeavor you're undertaking.

That means you are willing to pay the price, put in the time, wake up before others, and forgo some the easy pleasures of life that can distract you from preparation and relentless practice. You will develop a dogmatic commitment that drives you to do and accomplish goals you could hardly imagine accomplishing.

If you're wondering how I did in wrestling, I took the silver medal.

Here's the difference: wrestling is a sport I had spent years preparing for. I had learned everything I could at that time about the sport of wrestling. It was a sport I was committed to. Over the years, I had invested thousands of hours in hot, sweaty, stinky weight and wrestling rooms.

Will you go for excellence or mediocrity? It's your choice. Are you playing ping-pong thinking you might have a chance to win a few games but still needing to learn an astronomical amount about the sport? Or are you wrestling, very realistically competing for a medal? What I learned that day at the ping-pong table was that excellence requires commitment and preparation. Without them, you will always be mediocre.

Pearl S. Buck summed it up when she said, "The secret of joy and work is contained in one word: excellence. To know how to do something well is to enjoy it."[34] Leaders know that doing something well, with the benefit of consistent learning, is one of the most gratifying things there is.

Critical Leadership Characteristics

Ask any headhunter or executive recruiter: one of the rarest qualities in interviewed candidates is the capacity to continually reinvent organizations so they can thrive in our ever-changing business environment. For leaders to grow their organizations, they must become not only learning leaders but also teaching leaders. The same applies to the leader of a family.

The entire team, especially the leaders of those teams, must pass their wisdom on to others. Learning leaders embrace and enjoy teaching, coaching, and mentoring others. They develop an organization that is not satisfied with the status quo. They challenge the traditional method of doing things, and in the process, they develop more efficient and effective processes, solutions, and products. Since learning is vital to the success of any organization, true leaders set aside the time and develop tactics for their "troops" to learn daily.

Strong leaders are strong instructors and co-learners. Companies that succeed long-term succeed because they endlessly teach, train, and rejuvenate the leadership team at every level of the organization. Leaders look for productive ways to find teaching opportunities, and they turn each interaction with their troops into a learning and teaching experience. They are hired to build people, not simply organizations.

If you think I am talking just business here, think again. These critical leadership characteristics hold true in any organization. I don't care if you are a coach of a local youth athletic team, a single father of four, a teacher in a room full of eight-year-olds, or the patrol leader of your local Scout troop. If you are going to transcend mere management, you must cultivate a love for learning.

One of the most crucial aspects of learning is perspective—and if you want to be a powerful and impactful leader, you need to constantly adjust yours. The importance of that was brought home to me the day my youngest daughter wore her first pair of glasses. As I drove her to school, she marveled at the clarity and her new perspective of her surroundings. She was wide-eyed and excited to see her world in vivid, living color.

"Dad, I can see every blade of grass."

"Dad, I had no idea there were so many leaves on the trees and that they were so green."

"Dad, look at that sign; I can read it from clear back here. I had no idea my eyes were so bad."

It was incredible—until the next weekend when her glasses broke.

I'd rarely seen her so upset. And she came to me for help in fixing the problem.

I looked at her glasses and reassured her that it would be an easy fix—just a touch of Super Glue, and they would be good as new. Early Sunday morning, I sat down to fix her glasses. And I did a damn good job of it until the tiniest dab of glue got smudged across one of the lenses.

As she tried the glasses on, she was heartbroken. Her perspective of the world had changed again—and this time, her view was blurrier and duller than ever. Luckily, with a bit of fingernail polish remover and some gentle elbow grease, we had it fixed.

It was a powerful experience.

Before my daughter had tried on those glasses for the first time, she had no idea her view of the world was so distorted. Her blurry world had been her reality; she didn't know any different. But then she got those glasses. The world didn't change, but her perspective did—and as a result, her reality changed with it.

When I smudged her new glasses, she went from a clear reality back to blurred distortion. The contrast was stark and disappointing. She would not rest until her new lenses were clean and the clear vision she had come to enjoy was restored.

Your perspective of others and of life in general is totally unique to you. No one will ever have the exact perspective you do because no one else has ever had the exact life experiences you have had.

And that's not all. Your perspective changes over time. Your viewpoint at age fifteen is entirely different from the one you'll have at age forty. If you are lucky, you will learn this VERY important life lesson: *your perspective does not equal truth.*

My daughter learned that life lesson instantly when she changed her lens—and thus her reality.

Perspective Doesn't Always Equal Truth

Many go through life thinking their ideas, judgments, and beliefs about all kinds of things—including people, politics, or religion—are absolutely correct. What a perplexing palaver:

technically they are wrong, and yet they are right. Your perspective is *your* reality. So your perspective is *your* truth—but it's *not* everyone else's truth. Simple example: you may choose to see your backyard as a large swath of deep green with few details; that's your truth. But your neighbor may see the individual blades of grass that make up that large green lawn. That's his truth.

In other words, we are all living in the same world, and we are all looking at the same scenery, but how we perceive things can be completely different.

Your perspective does not always equal truth. Once you accept and understand this, amazing things start to take place in your own personal life. First, you're able to view circumstances and people from an objective, third-person outlook instead of being entrenched in "your" reality or "your" truth. Because of your ability to see multiple sides of an issue, you will no longer label people or circumstances as right and wrong, good or bad, saint or sinner, black or white. Instead, you will be able to practice deep empathy; you will understand the other person's ideas and beliefs without necessarily embracing them. And you'll be able to see the bigger picture when you combine perspectives.

You will see that each person has his or her own unique viewpoint and that, technically, that viewpoint is "right." It all depends on the lenses people are wearing. My daughter perceives the grass in her own way; if she is not wearing glasses, her reality will not equal truth.

Some people are able to look at issues or beliefs from multiple points of view and can empathize with those who see only one version. But you will also meet those who are fully fixed on the way they perceive things; these people cannot bring themselves to see a situation from any other point of view.

Either way, it's okay. People can only understand and process situations using the perspective they currently have. You can accept the situation only as it is because you'll never be able to convince them otherwise.

Every person you meet is *exactly* where he or she needs to be on his or her life's journey. The sooner you realize this, the sooner you stop the Sisyphean nightmare of trying to change people to meet your standards, *your* expectations, *your* reality, or *your* truth.

There's another blessing of realizing that your perspective does not always equal truth: it gives you the power to change your perspective at any given time, thereby letting you change your reality. If you don't like how something has happened, all you need to do is change your perspective of the situation. Instead of being a victim of circumstance, take control of your life. In *Don't Just Manage—Lead!* I wrote: "You see the world not as *it* is, but rather as *you* are" (35). That truism will always apply to our daily lives.

The people with whom I like to associate are those who seem to always see the best in others and the good in every situation. We all encounter situations that can cause us to feel angry, jealous, or bitter. But if you stay focused on the fact that every challenge is given to help you work through a weak aspect of your character or to magnify a limited belief system, you will allow yourself to find the silver lining in every cloud.

Challenge and question your current beliefs. Play with different lenses; look at your world from various perspectives. By doing so, you might not change what exists, but you will most definitely change your reality—and, as a result, your life. You will become more accepting of others and the events in your life, and you will no longer struggle with fallen expectations or people who see the world differently than you do. A beautiful inner peace will begin to grow and develop as you recognize and overcome your innate, limited perspectives. You will see that there *are* individual blades of grass and leaves on trees.

There is detail and beauty in everyone and every situation if you are willing to accept the fact that *your truth is not always reality* and that *you can change your lens of perspective* if you don't like your view.

Loving and Leading Are Linked

So, what about the final *L* in the concoction? Let's look at how loving is related to leading.

When I think of love, I think of unselfish service. For me, the ultimate act of demonstrating love is to serve others. If that's true, could being servant and leader be the same? Yes. You can be a leader who serves and a servant who leads.

Wait a minute, you may be saying. The words *servant* and *leader* seem to be on opposite ends of the spectrum—at least that may be how you've always understood things. They may even be seen as conflicting with each other. But that's the beauty in it: when two conflicting ideas, personalities, perspectives, or worlds come together, a compelling contradiction can be established.

In today's world, love and leadership go hand in hand. Let me say this loud and clear: you'll never be a great leader without being loving, empathetic, and compassionate. You cannot have leadership without love or love without service. Leadership is love via service.

I like to use the term *servant leader* to describe what I'm talking about. Being a servant leader implies a focus on putting others' needs, interests, and welfare above your own. It is an all-inclusive way of viewing the organization you lead—be it a corporate entity, a Little League baseball team, a Scout patrol, or a family. With a servant leader in charge, the interests and welfare of the whole supersede the interests of any one individual. Servant leaders check their ego at the door, and decision-making is shared as a team.

The servant-leader theory was pioneered in the seventies by Robert Greenleaf, a manager at AT&T. His paper "The Leader as Servant" started a drastic change in how organizations thought about leadership and the qualities leadership signified. According to Greenleaf, great leaders place service to others above any other responsibility on their to-do lists. Service is the foundation of their every endeavor. The service they render is the fuel that gives their leadership power and energy. Without service, they simply would not lead. Real leadership surfaces when those at any level in an organization are inspired to serve others. The same principles apply whether you are a younger sister serving your brother, a manager serving your peers, or an executive serving the receptionist. Service to team members, customers, neighbors, subordinates, or superiors is the principal focus and importance.

In *Don't Just Manage—Lead!* I clearly delineate between managers and leaders. A manager loves, thrives, and insists on complete control. In contrast, servant leaders defer their need for managerial control. Servant leaders admit and recognize that they do not have all the answers and that working holistically as a team leverages everyone's experience, expertise, and knowledge. It's not just the most optimal way forward, it is the *only* way forward in the long run.

It's been awhile since I've walked the halls of higher academia studying business management. Nevertheless, I remember courses on general business strategy, accounting, finance, marketing, sales, logistics, operations, corporate law, organizational behavior, analytics, communications, economics, manufacturing, international business, advertising, ethics, entrepreneurialism, and leadership itself. But I do not remember a single class that touched on the concept of love as it relates to leadership. In fact, had I asked fellow students or even professors back then about love and its role in leadership, they probably would have looked at me as if I had three heads.

If we want to connect as leaders, we must foster and develop a love of loving. Before you decide this is way too mushy, gooey, and squishy for you, I want you to stop. Stop and suspend those skeptical, cynical, logical thoughts and listen to your heart instead. Here's one reason: Learning to be a true servant leader may just change your life, and you may be the catalyst of change in your team or family. And your team's loving leadership may change the organization, and your organization may change your nation, and your nation may change the world.

Think I'm being melodramatic? Don't go there. Please stop rolling your eyes, and let's dive a bit deeper into the concept of love and leadership. In the next few pages, I want to explore the tender side of leadership: humility, compassion, kindness, and empathy—in other words, love.

I have shared my definition of a true leader in countless presentations. Please allow me to give it here:

Leaders offer visionary inspiration, motivation, and direction. Leaders create an emotional connection between themselves and the people they lead. Leaders attract people and build confidence and trust. Leaders ignite those they lead to put forth an incredible effort in a common cause, typically against uncommon odds. A leader leads with empathy, compassion, understanding, and a soft heart. All too often we think of leaders as stoic, tough, emotionally barren individuals who never cry, hurt, struggle, or laugh. For me, that's not a true leader. A true leader shows emotion, sheds a tear, apologizes for making a mistake, and admits when he or she doesn't know something. True leaders are vulnerable—and in that authentic vulnerability lies the incredible strength toward which others gravitate.[35]

As you read my definition, you will see that true leadership is not self-centered or arrogant—what we often call "my way or the highway." Leadership is much bigger than any one individual. You may have a title, you may have the office and the plaque on the door, and you may think of yourself as a leader—but if you are not obsessively passionate about serving others and watching them laugh, learn, love, and grow, you are no real leader. Leadership is about empathetically knowing your team, knowing your objective, and doing everything within your power to help your team succeed and meet that objective. Leadership has nothing to do with arrogance, pride, ego, or greed. These narcissistic qualities and desires only foster disconnection, distrust, disbelief, and isolated individualism.

Leadership is love.

Is it that simple? Let's put it to a quick test. Think about the great leaders with whom you have had the privilege of living, working, or being around for a time. Of those great leaders, how many were thoughtful, kind, caring, humble, and loving individuals? How many would bend over backward to take your call after hours, help you finish a project, or talk to you with respect, dignity, and politeness, no matter the situation? I am betting the great leaders that came to the top of your mind were trustworthy, fun, hardworking, vulnerable, kind people you would follow to the ends of the earth. These leaders are fun to be around as they spin off energy, ideas, and a positive vibe. With each interaction, they leave you feeling reinvigorated, focused, and motivated. You aren't pressured or forced to go the extra mile for these leaders—you go the extra mile because you are inspired to. You see the vision, you share the vision, and you are committed to making the vision a reality.

But let's not leave it there. Take a few moments to imagine one or more of the many not-so-great leaders you have had to endure. My guess is that they had wild mood swings and were relatively unpredictable. You never knew what you were going to get as they walked into the office, home, or locker room. Think about it: they always had an ulterior motive. If they seemed to be nice to someone, it didn't take long for you—and everyone else—to understand the real reason. It wasn't merely because they were nice. Quite the opposite.

When they worked toward an achievement, it wasn't for the team but rather for them. They may have *talked* about the importance of the team, but their words were rarely in alignment with their actions. They focused heavily on numbers alone, often putting the wins and losses, profit and loss, or their own reputation above everything else. There was a lack of trust, and you and your peers probably felt like mere assets. And everyone knew those assets could be made redundant or obsolete at any moment.

Were those not-so-great leaders kind, fun, vulnerable, humble individuals you truly wanted to be with? Not even close. They were regularly stressed, tense, and anxious, making everyone around them feel the same. When they wanted something done, they reverted to relentless pressure, bulldozing, and scoffing at any competing idea from others. Then, when the CEO, chairman of the board or press was around, they quickly slipped on a mask of calm, soothing smiles—even though everyone else knew better. Starting to get the picture?

Are great leaders strong? Absolutely. Humility, kindness, and empathy are not at odds with being tough. In fact, it is just the opposite. Some of the strongest leaders I know are the most compassionate leaders. Then why do so many leaders struggle to show their soft side? Why do so many see tenderness as a weakness and not a strength? I think it's because they are simply emulating those they have seen before.

What about the tough, SOB leaders you respected but didn't love? What about them? Easy—they were great managers, but they were not leaders. And as you undoubtedly know by now, managers and leaders are *not* the same.

Some may reluctantly try to lead because they feel it's expected of them. But they can carry that weight only so far. Over time they will either learn to love those they lead through service, or they will grow tired, cynical, or bored.

You cannot be strong-armed into leadership. It has to be something you want to do deep within your core. Your desire to serve must be authentic. The leader who is focused on serving others will seldom lose perspective and rarely veer from the main objective. If you are motivated for your own personal gain, you may achieve some intermediate successes, but in the long run, you will lose. History is full of leaders—both praised and forgotten—whose leadership skills didn't stand the test of time.

The bottom line is that leaders who focus on their people above the profits will, in the long run, be more respected and trusted, they will hold the loyalty of those they lead and ironically generate better long-term financial results.

Take Out Your Trash

A good leader loves in a way that is personal and real. A good leader is authentic. A good leader never stops to worry what others think of him; he is much more worried about what he thinks of others.

To show you how this works, I'm going to step up and use myself as an example.

Time for me to get personal and real.

What do I mean by that?

In her book *The Gifts of Imperfection,* Brené Brown, one of my favorite thinkers, authors, and speakers, calls it living a wholehearted, authentic life. She outlines what she calls her "10 Guideposts for Wholehearted Living":

1. Cultivating authenticity—letting go of what people think
2. Cultivating self-compassion—letting go of perfectionism

3. Cultivating a resilient spirit—letting go of numbing and powerlessness
4. Cultivating gratitude and joy—letting go of scarcity
5. Cultivating intuition and trusting faith—letting go of the need for certainty
6. Cultivating creativity—letting go of comparison
7. Cultivating play and rest—letting go of exhaustion as a status symbol and productivity as self-worth
8. Cultivating calm and stillness—letting go of anxiety as a lifestyle
9. Cultivating meaningful work—letting go of self-doubt and "supposed to"
10. Cultivating laughter, song, and dance—letting go of being cool and "always in control."[36]

You could fill libraries with thoughts on Brown's ten guideposts. But I want to focus on her first two. And in doing so, I want to get personal and real. By getting authentic with you, I'm going to shed any misconceptions that I am perfect. It's the same thing *you* need to do if you're going to be a loving, authentic leader.

I admit that at times I have evaded personal, real, and authentic as if that condition were the bubonic plague. Why? Sometimes I feel as though I have lived behind a carefully constructed mask, never letting anyone see the real me. That's often pretty handy, because if no one can see the real me, no one can dislike the real me.

Real is real. It is the kind of vulnerable honesty you try to hide from others—yet it is always there, staring back at you when you look in the mirror at the end of a long day and the mask inevitably crashes to the floor. Real is the raw truth—the trash you carry around while trying to hide it from others. It is hard enough to carry your trash day in and day out, but trying to hide it makes it even more difficult. Putting a mask on your trash only attracts more trash.

Want to know a secret? Others can see right through it. We all know you have trash. Worse yet, you all know *I* have trash. And guess what? I couldn't give a rat's ass whether you read it, judge it, talk about it, or even care about it. You shouldn't care what people think about your trash either. It was Coco Chanel who said, "I don't care what you think about me. I don't think about you at all." If you want to build self-esteem, which is a critical quality for loving servant leaders, it is vital to focus on your successes and shed your trash.

Here's a novel idea: for many years my self-esteem hasn't been self-esteem at all. If it were SELF-esteem, it would truly be based on *self*—on me and my opinions. But that's not what has been going on. Instead, I had been allowing the opinions of others to increase or decrease my self-esteem. Hence the mask.

I have been allowing OTHERS to determine my SELF-esteem? Does that make any sense? That's not self-esteem. That is parent esteem, neighbor esteem, spouse esteem, clergyman esteem, society esteem, associate esteem, stranger esteem—you name it. And you get the idea. Forging your way through life hiding behind a mask is anything *but* SELF-esteem.

My true self-esteem is based on *my* view of me, not on the opinions of others. Authentic self-esteem isn't reliant on what others think. And now you understand guidepost 1.

While I am always striving for improvement, it is continual *progress* I seek, not perfection. And that brings us to guidepost 2.

I was recently asked to speak at a conference for customer-care professionals. As the conference organizers were pulling together the flyer to send their members, they included my picture, my professional bio, and a blurb about the topics I would be discussing. It was the normal stuff you typically expect to see and read in the promotional material for a program such as this one.

I get it: They wanted to hype me as the keynote speaker. They wanted to build enthusiasm and excitement for the event. So my bio on the program read something like this:

Art Coombs is the founder, president, and CEO of KomBea Corp, a software company that develops call center software. Before founding KomBea, Mr. Coombs served as the EVP of Business Development/Strategic Initiatives for FirstSource, one of India's largest BPO/Contact Center Outsourcers. Before FirstSource, Art was CEO and founder of Echopass Corporation, which built the world's premier contact center hosting environment that was acquired by Genesys for more than $100 million. He also held various management roles with Sento Corp (SNTO), where he eventually became the CEO. Before Sento, Art served as managing director and vice president of European Business Development for Sykes Enterprises. Art is a published author of leadership, customer service, BPO/Contact Centers, outsourcing, and technical support methodologies. He is a recognized motivational speaker at conferences and corporate events around the world. Also, Art worked for organizations such as Hewlett-Packard, VLSI Research, and RasterOps.

When I read something like this—or, worse, listen to an events coordinator read it to introduce me—my eyebrows raise, my eyes roll, I grimace, my stomach tightens, and I want to shut down emotionally. I get sweaty, I feel anxious, and my brain seizes up. It is as if I were a *Peanuts* character sitting in Miss Othmar's class hearing, "Wah-wah-wah-wah" (translation: "Blah-blah-blah-blah-blah").

Why do I have this reaction? Is there something untrue in my bio? No—it is all true, and it accurately describes the vocational me. It is the truth many want to see. But it is such a skewed perspective of me.

What you just read in my bio is the truth that many rely on to measure, judge, and form opinions about me. It is a truth I can hide behind. In a way, it is my mask. To some, all of that stuff is important, and it signifies success. Then why don't I feel like a success?

Simple: vocational success is not the true level of success. I can always hear my father's maxim: "Genius is not being 'great' at any one thing. Genius is being 'good' in all aspects of your life. Genius is being good vocationally, socially, financially, physically, scholastically, emotionally, spiritually, and in your family." As a loving servant leader, you need to pay attention to all those areas.

Let's catch our breath and look at each of these categories. Let's get personal and real. I'll start!

Vocationally. You saw the bio. Everything in it is true. I'm good at what I do. I am not the brightest in the office, but I am bright enough to surround myself with mensa-level cohorts. I am blessed to work with some of the brightest, most loyal individuals to ever walk this earth. You may think I am hyperbolically exaggerating, but I love what I do and who I do it with.

Socially. As a kid, I was deathly shy, and I can still feel that shy little boy's painful awkwardness rise to the surface now and then. I prefer small, intimate groups over large crowds. But if I need to "work a large crowd," I can; I can be more extroverted if the occasion requires. I don't like to play games, so I'm not all that comfortable in large organizations where political correctness is a necessity. I have no interest in having my ass kissed *or* kicked by anyone but me.

Financially. I make a comfortable living, have a modest savings account, and have no debt. Most would think I am far better off than I am—but I will tell you that two divorces can knock you down a few rungs on the financial totem pole.

Physically. I love to work out—it's one of my go-to methods for dealing with stress. I strive to be healthy and eat a balanced diet, but I am not fanatic about it. (I admit I have an addiction to frozen Girl Scout Thin Mints.) I fight age aggressively yet naturally. Even so, I see the signs of age creeping up on me.

Scholastically. I was a deplorably low-performing high school student; in college, however, I was outstanding and graduated with honors. Why the massive turnaround? I have dyslexia, and it took me well into my twenties to understand, accept, and deal with it. I have many scholastic scars from ignorant teachers and peers who labeled me as "slow," "lazy," and "unintelligent." I had to come to grips with the reality of my dyslexia and how it affected me. I had to let go of what *others* thought of me and focus instead on what *I* thought of me. That led to the realization that I am *not* slow—far from it—but my mind works differently than others. Once I figured that all out,

I personalized how I approached my academic endeavors and was educationally set free.

Emotionally. Emotionally I am a work in progress. Like everything and everyone, I have my emotionally good days and my emotionally bad ones. I have days where sometimes I just want to run and hide; a thatched hut in the tops of the Himalayas would not be remote enough. When I am doing my old-man groove moves in the kitchen while lip-synching to a favorite song, my kids think I am a wreck. I'll admit there is a twisted side of me that enjoys being silly just to make them cringe with delight.

Spiritually. I was raised in a strict Christian home. My father and mother did not overtly push their religion on us, but there were unspoken—and at times spoken—expectations. While most of how I was spiritually raised was good and helped make me a better person, there were some downsides to it. A number of factors have tainted the positive spiritual feelings I once had: the relentless drive to be perfect (guidepost 2), the staggering shame placed on me when I wasn't perfect, what felt like the hypocritical judgment of others, and local religious leaders who at times were misguided, arrogant, and unethical. This internal dichotomy created an inner, pious ambiguity. While I still consider myself spiritual, I confess I am less religious.

Family. What can I say? I am an amazing father of four incredible children, yet I have been a deplorable husband. I struggle when dealing with big marital issues. I have been married twice and divorced twice. Yes, I am that piss-ant guy. My first marriage lasted sixteen years, my second twelve. Both ended in part because of my dishonesty. When the cardio and weights are not enough, my drug of choice is to find emotional validation elsewhere. Instead of stepping up like an authentically true, ardently secure man and addressing the issues, I cowardly practiced avoidance. While there are two sides to every pancake, this betrayal is entirely on me.

I know what I'm about to say sounds cliché, and I am not trying to make excuses or dodge the heat—but everyone makes mistakes. If you've made some yourself, just get up, dust yourself off, and vow to do better because of lessons learned. Vow to move forward, learn, laugh, love, and live.

So there you go—meet the real Art. The blemished, flawed, and human me. The Art few, if any, have ever seen. These are the terrifying, dark places I have masked for so many years. All that time, I have held back this self-disclosure because I was afraid of rejection. I presumed if others knew the real me, they would not like me. But that is not true. Not true at all.

To live balanced, authentic, real, wholehearted lives, we humans must connect with others. To connect on a meaningful level, we must take off our masks and tell our stories. We must be okay with our self-esteem because it truly is *our* self-esteem. And once we have self-esteem, as Leo Buscaglia says, "The easiest thing to be in the world is you. The most difficult thing to be is what other people want you to be. Don't let them put you in that position."[37]

Don't get me wrong: if you overload your family and friends with the mundane minutiae of all your personal trash, you will be tuned out as an emotionally weak, whiny loser. That, my, friend, will create separation—not connection. The critical piece to all this is being open, transparent, and humbly honest without being excessively needy.

Not only must you tell your story, you must allow others to tell theirs. You need to listen with empathy and love people unconditionally. It's vital to be tolerant and accepting of others even though you're not necessarily tolerant of their actions.

Many of us hold back from self-disclosure because we fear being rejected. Sometimes that fear is so intense it's the only thing we can see. Again, we reason, *If they knew the real me, they would not be interested in me!* But that's not true.

We are all exceptionally unique. The key to connecting with others—to being a loving servant leader—is being open, honest, and respectful with others and letting people know the real you. When you live your life unafraid of what others think of you, a fascinating thing happens. You find that when you're the authentic, real, wholehearted you, you attract authentic, real, wholehearted people.

If you really want to go the extra mile, take the categories I've listed and conduct your own life audit. No one else ever has to see it, so don't hold back, don't lie to yourself, and don't tell half-truths. Be honest with yourself about where you are. It's the only way to build the bridge to where you want to be.

No more masks—shed the trash! Let's get authentic.

Authenticity Paves the Way

Authentically great leaders are soft, fun, empathetic, and loving, and that allows them to be fair, approachable, and to demonstrate incredible will when called for. There's another important factor. Managers—of anything—focus on the *who, when, how,* and *where.* Leaders always include the *why.*

Walt Disney was a world-renowned, amazingly effective leader who focused on the why. As a result, a man named Floyd Norman became one of the world's top animators.

"Walt Disney did not always provide the answers for you. Ask anybody who has worked for Mr. Disney," Norman said. "He made it quite clear what he wanted and then our job was to deliver the goods. And so for a young kid like myself, working in story, to have a guy like Walt Disney . . . guiding you along the way, it was a . . . great opportunity to learn from a master, firsthand."

When you give individuals the why and they buy into it, stand back and get out of their way. Like Disney, let them figure out the how. They will accomplish amazing things with very little management because they will have become responsible managers of their own time and talents. Their morale will be higher, and they will be more enthusiastic and positive about what they are doing—all because you took the time to explain why.

The best way to explain the *why* is through personal anecdotes and stories. And great leaders are good storytellers.

Why are stories so important? They engage the emotional side of the brain and are the fuel that inspires others. Stories sidestep your critical thinking, influence you on an emotional level, and powerfully engage the intuitive portion of your brain. (And when you engage and stimulate that part of your brain, you think about the story and its meaning far longer.)

Accounts about you and your experiences are the most powerful because they're yours—and because you tell them with passion and poignancy.

Leaders communicate values through personal stories and anecdotes. It was Abraham Lincoln who said, "They say I tell a great many stories; I reckon I do, but I have found in the course of a long experience that common people, take them as they run, are more easily informed through the medium of a broad illustration than in any other way, and as to what the hypercritical few may think, I don't care."[38] If President Lincoln could save our nation and stop slavery while using personal stories and anecdotes, we can certainly build better companies, families, and teams by repeatedly telling personal stories and anecdotes.

Be a Storyteller

I am a storyteller. I also believe stories are the most powerful medium for teaching others. While data may cause you to think, it is not what motivates you to act. That is done when the story or emotional side of the equation is triggered. When the heart is convinced that the head has it right, we are motivated to move.

So I tell and write stories, many of them personal in nature. Not because I think I am anyone special but because I can tell these stories with passion and a personal perspective only I can bring.

I'd like to share a few of those stories with you. Here are two of my favorites.

Several years ago, I took my kids to church. Like most eight- and nine-year-olds, getting all gussied up and sitting through boring meetings is not on the top of their to-do lists. (In fact, I'm way older than nine, and many church services feel to me like voluntary euthanasia.)

That having been said, I believe an introduction to the spiritual side of life is important. I feel it is my parental responsibility to expose my kids to as much as possible, allowing them to learn, choose, and grow into well-rounded adults. My son Kai and my daughter Mackey like to appease their gray-haired, old father, so we go. The joy they feel afterward is a stark contrast to the strife and angst I feel beforehand.

One Sunday as they were giving me massive grief, I challenged them to try to find one positive thing during Sunday school that would make them a better person.

After Sunday school, I saw Kai standing in the hall with a grin on his face. I asked, "How was your lesson?"

He said, "I don't know; this is what I did instead." He then handed me a piece of paper. On it the following words were written in an oddly shaped column: Kind, brAve, faIthful, exCellent, Obedient, lOyal, awesoMe, Best, and honeSt.

"Wow," I said. "What a list of positive words!"

He looked at me and grinned. I quickly sensed I was not getting the entire story. He then asked, "Dad, do you know what it says?"

I looked at it again. Still wanting to stay positive and not deflate his enthusiasm, I asked, "Is this your attempt at the Scout Law?" I was prepared to help him fix it.

He smiled and said, "No, Dad. It is not the Scout Law—it is better."

I looked at the paper once more. All I saw was a list of positive adjectives written in a way that displayed awkward handwriting, capitalization, and formatting. I simply couldn't figure it out. He just kept beaming up at me. And I kept looking at the paper.

Then I saw it. It jumped up and slapped me in the face. There it was, big as life—my son affirming his self-worth in such a creative, clever way—using positive words to spell out his name with the capital letters in each word. I gave him a powerful man-hug.

I know I'm not completely objective here—and how can I be?—but what nine-year-old thinks like this? Talk about comprehending and crushing my challenge!

That leads me to my second story. A few years ago while coming home from church one Sunday morning, I asked Kai (ten at the time) and Mac (eight at the time) what they'd learned in Sunday school. Mac, sitting in the front seat—after all, she was first to get to the truck—animatedly showed me a picture she had colored. There were very few colors (the teacher's fault, I'm sure). Thrusting the paper at me, she blurted out, "We learned about Abraham and Isaac."

Mac has always been fascinated with the morbid, so I wasn't surprised when she added, "Oh yeah, Dad—look at the dagger in Abraham's hand. Did you know that Abraham was told to KILL his own son?"

I felt she was a little too obsessed with the gruesome nature of the thing, so I calmly said, "Yes, I know the story." All the while, I noticed Kai was being Kai—quietly sitting in the backseat, thinking. So I decided to engage him. Watching him in the rearview mirror, I asked, "Kai, did you also talk about the story of Abraham and Isaac in your class?"

Staring out the window and showing zero emotion, he mumbled, "Uh-huh."

I know my kids are different and their personalities are at times polar opposites, but my kids' dichotomous reaction to this biblical story captivated me. Mac was totally into it and mesmerized by the story. Kai seemed completely indifferent.

In an attempt to bring Kai into the discussion, refocus Mac's grisly obsession with the dagger, and hopefully drive home one of the more enlightening morals of the Abraham/Isaac story, I said, "Kai, think about it. What would you say if I said God told me to kill you?"

The truck went eerily silent for a second. (To be honest, it was hard for me to hear those words come out of my mouth.) Kai quickly looked up and calmly said, "Are you sure God didn't say AJ?" (AJ is Kai's older brother.)

As I watched in the rearview mirror, Kai—*so* smart and quick-witted—looked like a cat who had just caught a mouse. His grin was priceless. It took Mac and me several moments to register what he had said. Then we simultaneously burst out in laughter—all three of us. We laughed all the way home.

Whether it is a complex play on words or a witty, short quip, Kai reminds me time and time again that children are far more capable of understanding complex, deep issues if we just take the time to teach them—or, as it was in my case, let them teach us.

I *know* my children are capable of grasping far more complexity than I realize. I have a tendency to give my children short, watered-down facts without explanations—I tell them the *how, who, what,* and *when,* but I often leave out the *why.* What my children continually teach me is that I can and ought to give them the *why.* Giving them the why is often the hard part of parenting because it requires me to dig a bit deeper, take a bit more time, and exercise a lot more patience. It forces me to lead instead of merely manage.

So next time your children ask you a *why* question, give an answer that goes a little bit beyond a statement of fact and helps them understand the meaning behind what they're asking about.

As you strive to be a leader, remember the words of Harvey S. Firestone, the American businessman who founded the Firestone Tire and Rubber Company, one of the first global makers of automobile tires. He said, "The growth and development of people is the highest calling of leadership."[39] What he was saying, in other words, is that learning, laughing, living, and loving are an important collection of tools for any leader.

Henry Kissinger, an American diplomat who served as secretary of state under President Richard Nixon, said it this way: "The task of the leader is to get his people from where they are to where they have not been."[40]

With what you'll learn in the rest of this book, you will be able to do exactly that.

CHAPTER 4

Loving: The Very Essence of Connection

"I have found that if you love life, life will love you back."[41]

—Arthur Rubinstein

IT WAS the legendary Beatles songwriter and guitarist who put it out there—bold, simple, and true. If you want to be genuinely connected to another human being, all you need is love.

That's right. Love is all you need.

Sounds simple, but in its simplicity, it is very complicated.

From the beginning of time, mountains have been climbed, oceans explored, kingdoms established and defended, cities built, and wars fought, all because of love. Families have been established and children created as a result of love—yet murders and suicides have also been committed under the guise of that same sentiment. It is the simplest and most sublime of human emotions, yet it can be the most complex.

It is one of the most studied topics in all of history. Socrates, Plato, and Aristotle, among other ancient truth seekers and philosophers, discussed and debated the meaning of love. Shakespeare, Frost, Whitman, and Dickens are among the many whose sonnets explore and celebrate this most transcendent emotion. There are endless poems on the topic. Entire libraries could be filled with books on love alone. And music? The Beach Boys, Beatles, Everly Brothers, Ella Fitzgerald, Elvis Presley, Frank Sinatra, Nat King Cole, Madonna, Maroon5, and every other artist you can name has taken a whack at it. In fact, your MP3 player doesn't come close to having the capacity to store all the tunes there are about love.

Because of all that, you may think you know all there is to know about love. At the very least, you may think you've heard all you need to hear. You may even want to dismiss it because you figure it's too damn sentimental, mushy, or sloppy.

Wait!

Give me a chance here. I want to tackle love head-on. I want to dive right in and explore the topic in a way that may just give you a moment's pause—a way of looking at it as you've never seen it before. And the reason is simple: the world needs love as it never has before. *You* need love as you never have before.

Why? Because love is the most powerful connection possible between people. It is the thing that ultimately brings each of us—you, me, and everyone else—joy and purpose in living. Johann Wolfgang von Goethe, the writer and philosopher considered Germany's greatest man of letters, put it this way: "The world is so empty if one thinks only of mountains, rivers, and cities; but to know someone who thinks and feels with us, and who, though distant, is close to us in spirit, this makes the earth for us an inhabited garden."[42]

So stick with me while I go to bat for love.

Love Thy Self

Let's start at the very beginning: love of self. Research professor and best-selling author Brené Brown wrote, "Love is not something we give or get; it is something that we nurture and grow, a connection that can only be cultivated between two people when it exists within each one of them—we can only love others as much as we love ourselves."[43]

She hit the nail right on the head. There are so many ways to say it. If you don't love yourself, it's impossible to love someone else. If you don't know it, you can't teach it. You can't give someone else what you don't possess yourself. You can't spin off loving energy if that loving energy isn't spinning within.

If you're empty, you can't seek the love of someone else to fill your void. It doesn't work that way. If your happiness depends on someone else, please go back to square one and take a serious look at what's going on in your heart.

Simply put, love of self is the inner estimate of what you think of yourself. It's an audit you do of your own emotional bank account. You've probably heard it called by a number of different names: *self-respect, self-worth, self-confidence,* and *self-esteem* among them. But all of those describe the same thing: love of self—an optimistic, confident, and upbeat way of visualizing yourself.

There are certain hallmarks of healthy self-love. You value yourself as well as others. You clearly see your strengths as well as your weaknesses, and you focus on those strengths as a way to accomplish the things that are important to you. While you're well aware that life has its share of bumps, potholes, and detours, you never give up or abandon your goals. You're able to do things well because what you do is a natural reflection of the way you feel about yourself.

Healthy self-love causes you to focus far more on what *you* think and feel than on what others think and feel about you. You display a calm confidence that is evident in your cheerful smile and quick wit. You do what is right because you know it is right, and you take joy in performing anonymous acts of kindness. You often share loving energy with those who need it because you have more than enough loving energy in your emotional bank account. Or as Gautama Buddha says, "You can search throughout the entire universe for someone who is more deserving of your love and affection than you are yourself, and that person is not to be found anywhere. You yourself, as much as anybody in the entire universe deserve your love and affection."[44]

When you have plenty of self-love, sharing it with others can be as easy as writing a simple note. I'll never forget what happened while I was busy flipping burgers one day.

For the past twenty-plus years, I've enjoyed a great tradition at my children's schools: every year I've hosted a barbecue for my kids and their classes. I pick a day in May near the end of the year, haul in my grills, and treat the students and faculty to a day of fun and celebration. I love watching the kids excitedly eat, play, sing, and dance as I loudly play some appropriate tunes to set the mood.

At one barbecue, something happened that had never happened before: one of the teachers wrote a thank-you card and discreetly handed it to me while I was fixing her hamburger.

I was stunned.

In more than twenty years, no one had ever written me a thank-you note. Sure, almost everyone I fed in all those years verbally expressed gratitude for the food and my efforts to provide it. But this one teacher alone went the extra mile and took time to express her thanks by handwriting a thoughtful and heartwarming message. It was a manifestation of her love of self.

I slipped the small envelope into my back pocket and went on serving food to the faculty and students. Only later did I have an opportunity to read it. A few days later I reached out to her and thanked her for the thanks. Then she thanked me for thanking her for thanking me. The thanking just kept going, and it made us both laugh. But the truth is her small, proactive gesture made me think: How many times do we feel positive toward another person yet fail to express appreciation? How often do we pass up the opportunity to connect on a meaningful level?

Any note, of course, is a real step in the right direction, but a *handwritten* note is particularly powerful. Think about it: I have personally saved many handwritten notes and cards from bosses, peers, friends, children, parents, and others—but with rare exception do I ever save a text or email, no matter how poignant or personal. Handwritten notes may take more time, may not be as neat and tidy, and may take longer to reach your reader, but the power of personal touch will make a far deeper impression than the same thought quickly shot off in an email or instant message. It's one of the best ways you can connect with and demonstrate your love for another soul.

Pay It Forward

Whenever I think of healthy self-love and its expression, I also think of the concept known as "pay it forward."

Unless you've been hibernating or in a self-induced coma for the past two or three decades, you've heard the expression. There have been books, films, and endless blogs on the subject.

The premise is simple. "Pay it forward" means that when someone does a good deed for you, you pass it on—you do a good deed for someone else. When it works as it should, it starts a veritable snowball of good deeds rolling, gathering power as it goes. People connect; good things happen. And the very best good deeds are the secret ones.

I am a devoted advocate of the "pay it forward" philosophy. And whenever I think about it, I remember a great example from about ten years ago when my son AJ and I stopped at a local gas station. While there, we filled my truck with diesel and popped in to get a drink. As we were at the soda dispenser (yes, I know there are healthier drink options), I noticed two rather young-looking police officers walk in. I thought, *Man, those guys have a tough job, and I am so grateful they are the ones doing it instead of me.* I know there are bad apples in every bunch, but every law enforcement officer I have ever met has been a decent person, trying his or her best to make the community safer for everyone.

As AJ and I got in line to pay for our drinks, the officers got in line a few customers behind us. As I stepped up to the counter, I whispered to the young clerk to visually scan what the officers had and to add it to my total. As it turns out, it was like some scripted, cliché cop movie: they each had a donut and a large soda.

The clerk smiled, clearly enjoying our covert operation of kindness, as he added about five dollars to my bill. I paid, we made our way back to the truck, and we were on our way. So far, so good—it was the perfect, anonymous, secret good-deed caper. Though things were about to change, it still didn't take away from the experience.

Here's what happened next. We were about two blocks away when I glanced in my rearview mirror. My heart stopped. There was not one, but *two* patrol cars following me, lights pulsing. I hate that initial feeling; seeing those lights spinning and flashing behind me always inspires instant anxiety, just as I'm sure it does for you.

As I pulled over and started collecting my license, registration, and insurance information, I glanced in the side mirror and noticed that the officers getting out of their cars were the same officers I had just stealthily purchased donuts and drinks for. Why were they stopping me? My mind raced. Did the clerk divulge us as the good-deed doers, and did the officers simply want to say thanks? Or wait—had I been speeding? Did I miss the light a block back? Great.

As one officer approached my door, the other meticulously scanned the back-passenger seat and carefully watched my son from the other side of the truck. I rolled down my window, and the officer autocratically demanded, "License and registration." There was no pleasant chitchat; he didn't even say *please*.

Wow, I thought, *they really mean business. I wonder what the problem is.*

After the officer looked at my license, he glanced up and asked, "Do you know why we pulled you over?"

"No, Officer, I honestly don't have a clue."

"Your registration expired six months ago."

I had no idea. It was a simple oversight.

But he wasn't finished. "Is this your truck?"

I suddenly realized that they suspected they might have a stolen vehicle on their hands.

"Officer, I promise," I stammered. "I simply forgot about the registration. I paid for the truck; it is mine."

With a crusty, distrustful look, he took my license and expired registration and said, "I will be back in a moment. You stay here."

As he turned and began walking back to his car, I said, "How are those drinks and donuts?"

He stopped dead in his tracks. As he turned back and walked up to me, I could see that his expression was totally different. Instead of a cautious, wary-eyed suspicion, a smile spread across his face and demonstrated his youthful age.

"Sir, are you the one who paid for our drinks and donuts back there at the convenience store?"

"Yes, Officer. That was us." (Sometimes it's smart to confess!)

With that, he yelled across the truck to his partner. "Case closed. I know who paid for our snacks." They both started to laugh. "Sir, how in the world can I issue you a citation after what you did?"

As he handed back my license and lapsed registration, I promised to get my truck registered immediately, and he and his partner expressed how grateful they were for our small act of kindness. As my son and I drove away, I thought, *Wow—I have never seen the positive effects of paying it forward boomerang so rapidly!* It provided a perfect opportunity for my son and I to talk about the "Pay It Forward" maxim and how doing kind acts of kindness often has a unique way of boomeranging back to you.

We'd spent five bucks on some simple donuts and sodas and created a positive energy that was produced for the clerk at the counter, those in line who overheard and observed, my son and I, as well as the police officers. For just five bucks and a little effort, we all had a dose of goodness, positivity, and feeling uplifted. Yes, we got out of a citation, but the positive karma that was produced for all involved was far more valuable. The tiniest act of anonymous kindness is worth more than any of the attention, applause, or accolades some seem to crave. Love, tolerance, and kindness build bridges of understanding, acceptance, and friendship. On the other hand, anger, greed, and hate build walls of distrust, fear, and disconnection. I could have given a million parental sermons to my son, but having him watch firsthand what can happen when you show kindness was far more powerful.

Let's face it—we all struggle. We all have those down moments. But, fortunately, we also all have up moments—moments when we experience love, peace, and joy. As humans, we can't help but love. It's part of our being human.

When we start to drown in our sorrows, we all too often turn inward and lose sight of the needs of those around us. We simply go into self-preservation mode. It's important to take care of yourself; you can't save others if you feel like you are drowning. That's an important part of healthy self-love. But it's also vital to look outside ourselves at the same time and see the need in others. It may be challenging, but it's an instant, palpable boost to our feelings of self-worth.

It takes only one act of kindness to profoundly affect your mood and lift your sinking spirits. Think about the "kind acts" others have performed on your behalf. Remember the driver who let you in on the freeway with a wave and a smile? Think of the person in the checkout line who let you go first because you had only a few items while she was stocking up for Armageddon.

Studies have shown that random, anonymous acts of kindness are good for you! They improve your life satisfaction by increasing your sense of self-worth. They improve your health by decreasing your anxiety, depression, and blood pressure. Think how amazing that is: kind acts benefit not only the recipient, they also benefit the doer of the deed and everyone who observes the deed along the way. Every act of kindness improves the lives of many. Best of all, every act of kindness is another strong element in the connection that binds us all and in the development of healthy self-love.

So buy someone soda and a donut today. Put me to the test. I guarantee it works. Pay it forward—you will be happier and less stressed when you make someone's day a touch brighter, and you'll enjoy a new sense of connection through it all.

See the Worth in Everyone

There are other qualities that demonstrate healthy self-love. Bolstered by an appropriate love of self, you move through life in a way that attracts and inspires others. People instinctively trust you; you are unusually good at solving problems and typically make good decisions. While you ask others for input and weigh those viewpoints thoughtfully, you're not intimidated by differing opinions, and you own your choices. You dig deep in search of solutions, and you ultimately get where you want to be.

Healthy self-love fuels an inner happiness that tends to even out life's good and bad, ups and downs, rights and wrongs, highs and lows, victories and defeats. It inspires you to learn and explore new talents, hobbies, and interests. You're rarely bored; instead, you are creative in many ways and have a sense of wonder about the things around you. When you love yourself in the right way, you find your life distinguished by lots of smiles, laughter, and joy.

Perhaps most telling, when you have a profound sense of self-love, you share respectful and loving relationships with others. Because you see the worth in yourself, you can see it in others. You trust and love others because you trust and love yourself.

A wonderful example of this very concept is one I remember with great fondness—not only because of the trust and love it exemplified on the part of all involved, but because it was so funny. My son AJ is now in his early twenties and is a responsible, thoroughly enjoyable young adult. Though he has moved several states away, I love talking to him and spending time with him whenever I'm able. And that very gratifying experience sometimes makes me chuckle as I reflect on how much he's changed in just the last half decade.

I don't know about you and your kids, but mine could be a tad self-centered while they brooded through the teen years. On occasion, my teens saw me as not much more than a giving tree—doling out cash, cars, vacations, cell phones, food, and other niceties. Truthfully, that was okay with me—the fact that they needed me was exactly the hook I craved (and still crave) to stay connected and involved in their lives. You see, maybe just like what has happened to you, my kids started pulling away as they hit the teen years.

At the time, I worried that their pulling away was some sort of indictment on my parenting style or maybe their way of rebelling against an impending divorce. Now, with the blessing of hindsight, I realize it was a normal part of their development as they started experimenting with independence. I found out later that they all do it. I just didn't know it at the time. My sense of self-worth could have really used that bit of info.

As my children cruised into their midteens, their friends became a huge part of their universe. In fact, it seemed their entire lives centered on their friends. They did not necessarily care about dad time, mom time, or family time; they were totally preoccupied with their own time. Up against the priority of their friends, I saw them less and less often.

As we all pulled out of that stage, I realized that if I just stayed involved, I could build and sustain trust, love, and connection while simultaneously encouraging the independence critical at this stage in their lives. And that brings me to the experience I will always treasure.

It was a late Friday evening at about 5:30 p.m. I was in my office, wrapping up for the day. As I was getting ready to leave for home, I got a text from seventeen-year-old AJ.

It was pretty straightforward: "I got done with my chores early. Wanna go out?"

Now let's think about this for a few minutes.

First, it was a Friday night.

Second, the text came from my seventeen-year-old.

Third, he was asking me to "go out." It all seemed pretty uncharacteristic of my teenage son.

So as I read it, I was fairly certain the text was not meant for me, his dad. It had to be a mistake. He must have punched in the wrong number. Surely he'd meant to send the text to one of his friends—perhaps his girlfriend.

I decided to play a little joke on AJ. So I teasingly sent a text right back. My reply? "Sure, I would love to. How about we go dancing?"

I waited and waited and waited. I could see that he had read my text, and I wondered why he was not responding. Then it hit me. By then he must have figured out that he'd inadvertently sent that text to me. I figured he was probably laughing and trying to come up with a clever retort.

But as the minutes dragged by, I still heard nothing.

About five minutes later, my eldest daughter, Kelly, called me. In a very confused and kind of solemn voice, she asked, "Dad, why do you want to go out dancing with AJ?"

"What are you talking about?" Now *I* was the one who was confused.

She patiently described the facts. "AJ just called me and is freaking out because he says you want to go out dancing with him."

Things instantly became clear—or so I thought. I said, "Oh, you mean the text he accidentally sent me—the one that was meant for somebody else?"

I had barely taken a breath to start explaining my tongue-in-cheek response when Kelly interrupted me and said, "No, Dad. AJ sent it to *you*. He wants to go out with *you*—not his friends or his girlfriend."

I chuckled a bit, thinking about what must have been going through AJ's head when he got my reply. *What the heck is Dad talking about?* Dancing . . . *with Dad . . . Gross! The old man has absolutely lost it.*

But then I felt a warm glow in my heart that my seventeen-year-old son wanted to go out with his dad and siblings on a Friday night. We went bowling, had a blast, and then went out for pizza.

No silver-back gorilla had more pride. I love this crew.

I am no Steven Pinker, Brené Brown, or Paul Jenkins, but I am a father of four who has done a few things right. And through all those lessons in the school of hard knocks, I feel qualified to pass on these thoughts and suggestions: Parents (especially single parents), do not focus on the loss of time with your teens as they pull away. Focus on your self-worth and the worth you admire in them. Build bridges of trust, interest in common activities, and a strong, loving relationship early in their lives. That's the stuff of strong connections. If you kick in at the last minute and try to be the "parent" when the relationship with your teen is already strained from early neglect, you're going to have a very steep mountain to climb.

As they become teens, ditch the idea that you are losing their time, interest, and affection. Instead, focus your energy on maintaining a nurturing, positive, solid relationship as a demonstration of healthy self-love. Think long-term; the teen years are merely a stepping stone. Make sure those stones have a strong, loving foundation so the relationship can endure far into the future.

Establish good communication and be interested in being together. Celebrate life's ups and downs, traditions and holidays.

As my kids grow older, move out, and make lives of their own, I pray I have invested early enough and often enough in my relationship with them that they want to keep building it. I pray I have forged the kind of connection that will endure forever. You see, one day I hope to get a text from my grandson saying, "Grandpa, I got done with my chores early. Wanna go out?"

Avoiding Unhealthy Self-Love

As you can see, my experience with AJ was an awesome display of healthy self-love on both our parts. I hope you're starting to understand the concept, because it's critical to your ability to love others as well. If you're going to understand self-love, you also need to understand its opposite.

For example, sometimes it's easy to confuse the hallmarks of healthy self-love with the characteristics of an unhealthy self-image. For example, healthy self-love brings with it a calm confidence—which is *not* the same as the "let's talk about me" syndrome. Respecting and appreciating your own worth is *not* the same as being self-*centered* (or even narcissistic). Those with healthy self-love enjoy performing anonymous acts of kindness or service; and while those with shallow self-esteem might do things for others, they always find a way to discreetly take the credit—something that serves their need to be the hero, the knight in shining armor. At its worst, they use acts of kindness as tools of control and manipulation. It is always about *them, their* agenda, *their* interests, and *their* perceived happiness.

While those with healthy self-love enjoy respectful relationships with others, the opposite occurs in the face of unhealthy self-esteem. These people try to control and smother their partners; fueled by jealousy, they are distrustful about what the other person is doing, where they are going, and to whom they are talking. They may stalk their partner's social media friends, followers, and activity, trying to intercept phone calls, text messages, emails, and other forms of communication.

Paranoia is dialed up to its fullest for these folks. They trust no one. They believe everyone is out to get them and that everyone has an agenda or ulterior motive. Why? Because they themselves have agendas and ulterior motives. Again, "We see the world not as it is, but rather as we are." Nothing could be truer for those saddled with sagging self-esteem. They are always the victim, and they eagerly cast blame for any slight in every direction but their own. They feel justified and even correct in any type of bad behavior because it's always *someone else* that has provoked them.

It's relatively easy to spot someone who lacks healthy self-love. One of the quickest signs is radical mood swings: he is happy one minute, angry the next. She can be solemn, sad, and withdrawn until the doorbell rings—and then she's all smiles. The smallest things can set these people off, and those around them are constantly walking on eggshells in an effort to avoid an explosive outburst.

Another sign is frequent changes in employment. Those with unhealthy self-esteem often alienate themselves from others and literally work themselves out of a string of jobs. When bosses or colleagues have had enough of their bad behavior, the sorry victim will always try to turn things around to make themselves feel better: *I'm too smart for these idiots. These guys have no clue what they are doing. I'm too good for this place.*

Self-absorbed people go to great lengths to appear happy, secure, confident, and like they've got it together—especially to friends, neighbors, coworkers, and even casual acquaintances. But here's the problem: no one can keep up that kind of façade forever. And sadly, when the mask falls off and the pretense comes crashing down, it's the close family members—the spouse, children, and siblings—who are left trying to cope with a bitter, confused, imbalanced, possibly even violent person who seems smiling, carefree, and happy to those on the outside.

Okay, before you pick out a few mistakes you've made and decide to label yourself as a hopeless poster person for unhealthy self-esteem, stop right there. You have blemishes. I have them too. We all do. There isn't a day that passes when you don't do or say something foolish, inappropriate, or even stupid. That's the way it is for *everyone*. The key is to continue to make deposits in your emotional bank account—and to audit it consistently.

To show you what that means, I want to share a powerful metaphor. I've heard this story told in a number of different ways and by different people, but I like the version told by award-winning author Dr. Greg Bear best. His version helps me understand my own feelings whenever my emotions start to get the better of me—and then gives me the tools to maintain calm emotional stability and healthy self-worth.

Here's how it goes: Imagine you work your tail off doing a hard job and you earn one hundred dollars for your efforts. What a sweet sense of accomplishment! When you get home, you proudly place the hundred-dollar bill on the kitchen table while you wash up and get ready for dinner. Out of the corner of your eye, you see a visiting friend quickly pick up the money and stuff it in his pocket.

What? You *saw* it happen. There is no question who took your money and that it was intentional. It was Theft 101, plain and simple. How do you feel? What do you do?

Faced with this situation, most people say, "I'd be furious! I would aggressively address the situation at once and get that hundred dollars back! No one—not even a friend—is going to steal from me!"

Sound like how you'd feel? I'm betting it is.

Now let's change the scenario a little. Let's say you've worked for a long time and earned $100,000. When you are paid that glorious lump sum, you come home and (for some inexplicable reason) put it on the kitchen table. What a sweet sense of accomplishment! Pause for a moment and really try to imagine it: $100,000 in cash, all in hundred-dollar bills, stacked neatly on your kitchen table.

As you are washing up and getting ready for dinner, you see a visiting friend pluck a hundred-dollar bill from the top of one of the stacks and stuff it in his pocket.

Again, you *saw* it happen. There is no question who took your money and that it was intentional—it was Theft 101. How do you feel? What do you do?

Notice how your attitude changes. Instead of feeling angry and prepping for an explosive confrontation, most in this situation have feelings of empathy, benevolence, and concern for the friend who is obviously so desperate he must resort to stealing. Some say they'd compassionately ignore it altogether. Others say they'd still confront the friend—but this time with love, mercy, and tenderness, maybe even offering the friend another hundred if he needed it that desperately.

What changed?

The amount of money stolen was the same; a hundred dollars is a hundred dollars.

The two people didn't change; it's still you and your friend.

The only thing that changed was your perspective of self-worth. Your attitude toward the thief goes from anger to love because when you have a strong emotional bank account of self-worth, you come at life with an attitude of compassion, mercy, and empathy. If your emotional bank account is hovering near bankruptcy when it comes to self-worth and healthy self-love, you're more prone to fly off the handle, lose your cool, and resort to anger. So make sure your emotional bank account has a sizable balance. Do something every day to promote a healthy sense of love for yourself.

And that, of course, leads to the sublime experience of loving others, because loving others is an essential part of healthy self-love. As Jesuit priest and author John Joseph Powell wrote, "It is an absolute human certainty that no one can know his own beauty or perceive a sense of his own worth until it has been reflected back to him in the mirror of another loving, caring human being."[45] Most of us—including me—sometimes get tired of searching for love. It can be a road mired in nonstop twists and turns that leads to nothing more than a dead end. Some even despair of the notion that such a thing as genuine, unconditional love even exists.

Well, trust me. It does. But as I've learned from challenging events in my own life, sometimes we need to change our attitude and understanding of love so we can feel and experience that kind of love.

Believe me when I tell you that the work involved is well worth it. Trappist monk Thomas Merton, one of the most influential authors of the twentieth century, made this profound observation: "Love is our true destiny. We do not find the meaning of life by ourselves alone—we find it with another."[46]

Love Is . . .

Let's define it: *love is wanting the happiness of another with no ulterior motive.* When you love someone, there is no angle or agenda. You behave in a way that places that person's needs, wants, and wishes above your own. It defines how you treat others. It's not something that "happens to you"; it's how you happen to others. You control love—it does not control you.

Love is as natural as breathing. It has existed since the beginning of time and will be here long after we all depart. Every person on this earth has the ability to love and the desire to be loved, no matter their lot in life. Love is the driving force that allows our self-centered, egotistical side to look beyond our selfish needs and see others as fathers, mothers, sons, daughters, husbands, wives, brothers, sisters, coworkers and friends to be treasured, appreciated, and cherished instead of used, manipulated, and exploited for our own personal gain.

Love is love, irrespective of what we think it is. No matter how much we distort, trample, and twist the definition or essence of love, it never changes. Its nature is constant and endless regardless of our delusions, views, and imitations. Love does not care what society says it is, what you have been taught it is, or what you fantasize it is. Love is what you are and not what you selfishly want it to be.

It's probably important right now to make a critical distinction: *love is not the same as romance.* Sometimes love manifests itself as romance, but romance is not love. "Romance" dictates that you see the object of your romance as an idyllic image; when romance rules a relationship, you often insist on your partner changing to become what you want—to become the person you want him or her to be. Romance is inherently egotistical, and ego has no place in genuine love.

In fact, love is the polar opposite of self-absorbed ego. Let's be clear: love is not attention, power, security, entertainment, pleasure, or praise—self-centered attributes that are all external and ego driven. Real love is an intrinsic focus on the needs of others characterized by humility, goodness, and service.

I was lucky enough to be reared by two people who demonstrated exactly what love is—and they were still doing it during the twilight years of their lives. I saw a beautiful example of that in a place I least expected: driving through a sunset in a quiet German countryside.

Serenaded by Nat King Cole

While I was living in the Netherlands a couple of decades ago, my parents came for a visit. I decided to take them for a quick visit to Rothenburg ob der Tauber, one of my favorite little German towns about five hours by car from our home and just across the Dutch border.

Rothenburg is a popular, well-preserved medieval town located on what is called the "romantic road," which winds through Southern Germany. It is a quaint, picturesque little village that was spared from the carnage of the world wars. It's an absolute joy to visit and explore, so I thought it was the perfect place to take my parents for a quick overnight European excursion.

I arranged for a few days off, packed the car, and prepared to head out from our home in Holland. As I climbed into my Volvo sedan and prepared to set out on our journey, my father said, "Art, I think I will ride in the backseat with your mother." I'll never forget the warmth and gentleness in his voice. I quickly and happily agreed.

With me in the front and my parents in the back, I felt like an official tour guide; all I lacked was the black-and-white suit with its chauffeur's hat. As I stole occasional glances in the rearview mirror, I felt so grateful for my parents and their sweet relationship. They looked so cute sitting in the back, holding hands.

I was delighted to hear story after story from my parents as we drove through the Dutch and German countrysides. About two hours away from Rothenburg, the talking and storytelling began to wane; all three of us just enjoyed the scenery and the joy of simply being with each other.

I have very eclectic taste in music, and there are a lot of 1950s artists in my collection. One of my favorites is Nat King Cole. So when the conversation in the car died down, I slipped in my *Best of Nat King Cole* CD. Words can't describe my calm state of mind as I drove through the breathtaking scenery alive with the playful golden rays of the setting sun and listened to "The Very Thought of You," "Unforgettable," and other Nat King Cole classics while my parents snuggled in the backseat. With another glance in the rearview mirror, I saw that my father now had his arm around my mother and she was tenderly resting her head on his shoulder.

The sweet, mellow, loving energy in the car was indescribable. At that moment, Nat started in with "Tenderly." I can still hear the soulful lyrics and the catch in my father's voice as he quietly asked my mother, "Mignon, do you remember this song?"

I discreetly glanced in the rearview mirror and felt as though I were intruding on an intimate scene meant only for the two of them. My mother nodded, then quietly asked my father, "Do you remember that summer evening we were in the park the first time you kissed me?"

I could not keep from looking at them again, and my father's expression revealed the full measure of his memory and emotion. His eyes were red and moist. His lips were tight one instant and quivering with raw emotion the next as he relived this very intimate moment. Finally, he gently whispered, "This was one of our songs, Mignon. You are the best decision I ever made. I love you. Thank you."

My mother said nothing. She didn't have to. Her love for my father was more pure and obvious at that moment than I had ever witnessed.

I found myself transfixed, my own eyes moistening with emotion, a lump forming in my throat, my heart feeling ready to burst. I forced myself to stay focused on the road; we were, after all, on the notoriously fast German autobahn, and our safety demanded my focus. But that wasn't the only reason for my focus on the road: my parents were sharing a very intimate moment awash with loving memories, and I didn't want to interrupt it in any way. Nor did I want it to stop.

I had never heard much about my parents' courtship, and the scene playing out in the backseat was priceless. As the song began to fade to its last notes, I took one last quick peek in the mirror. I saw my parents giving each other a sweet, short kiss.

To this day, when I hear Nat King Cole sing his version of "Tenderly," I am instantly transported to that drive through the European countryside. I had the best seat in the house from which I witnessed a loving, unrehearsed story about my parents' song, their first kiss, and their affection for each other as they strolled through a park hand in hand, experiencing the first blush of young love.

This moment, this memory, this song, this story mean the world to me. Words fall woefully short when I try to describe the full measure of my emotions and the gratitude I feel for my parents and their willingness to let me be a part of their tender reminiscing. The small act of tender compassion I witnessed that late afternoon in Germany renewed my faith in human decency, civility, and true love.

As my parents demonstrated, to love quietly, powerfully, and consistently underscores the worth and beauty of others just the way they are. Love loves others without bias. Nobody believes, thinks, and lives exactly as you do, which is one of the most beautiful aspects of life. Real love does not insist everybody be exactly like you. There is no requirement that others have the same opinions, thoughts, beliefs, knowledge, or background. Real love embraces, encircles, and connects with others as they are.

Love Is Far More Powerful Than Bigotry

One of the most beautiful examples of such love I've ever heard of occurred in a very unlikely setting between two people who could not have been more different.

Many real-life Olympic celebrities were in attendance at the closing ceremonies of the National Explorer Olympics I attended in 1978. While waiting for the festivities to start, I ran up front and snapped a photo of decorated sprinter Jesse Owens and phenomenal swimmer John Naber. Getting the opportunity to see them, especially up close, was thrilling for a young, neophyte wrestler!

That night, I first heard a story that had tremendous impact on my life—probably one of the most influential examples of love I would ever hear. When it was his turn to take the podium, Jesse Owens told a true story that illustrates the finest qualities of love.

In 1936, the Olympics were hosted by Germany. At that time, Adolf Hitler and his Nazi regime were on the rise. For a time, the United States seriously considered boycotting the 1936 games in protest of Germany's aggression toward its neighboring countries. But in the end, the United States decided to participate.

Hitler and his Nazi cohorts thought Jews, African-Americans, and others were inferior to the white, Aryan race Germany was promoting with its hate propaganda. Many German leaders mocked America for allowing African-Americans to participate in the Olympics. One German official even complained that the Americans were letting "non-humans, like Owens and other Negro athletes" compete.

Hitler's well-known hatred of Jews and nonwhite races formed the background of the 1936 Olympics. Jesse Owens had to compete in a stadium thick with swastikas and straight-armed "Heil Hitler" salutes.

Owens won the gold medal in the hundred-meter dash. The next day, he participated in the long jump—an event in which he held the world record. Much to his disappointment, he foot-faulted on his first two qualifying jumps. If he fouled again, he'd be eliminated.

With only one jump remaining, Jesse was approached by Luz Long, the tall, blue-eyed, blond German long jumper who was Jesse's stiffest competition. Jesse was surprised when Luz encouraged him to do his best. In fact, he was stunned at this seemingly small but kind act of sportsmanship in the midst of the hatred being promoted by the German leaders.

On his third and final qualifying jump, Jesse advanced to the finals to compete against his new friend, Luz.

In the finals that afternoon, Luz's fifth jump matched Jesse's best. But Jesse then jumped farther, with a world-record jump of twenty-six feet, five-and-a-half inches. Jesse won the gold medal; Luz took silver.

Luz was the first person to run up and congratulate Jesse after his world-record leap. Jesse remembered that "Luz looked like the model Nazi, but wasn't."

Luz Long knew that his sportsmanlike gesture would not please Hitler, who sat prominently in the gathered multitude. But Luz publicly congratulated and embraced Jesse—then walked around the stadium with him, arm in arm, before an astonished German crowd.

Jesse recounted his feelings about the friendship Luz had displayed. He said, "You can melt down all the medals and cups I have, and they wouldn't be even a plating on the 24-karat friendship I felt for Luz Long at that moment."[47]

Adolf Hitler must have gone crazy watching one of his star athletes befriend an individual he thought inferior.

The sad part of the story is that Jesse and Luz never saw each other again. They did stay in contact and wrote several letters, but Luz was killed in World War II.

As a German soldier fighting in 1942, Luz wrote one last letter to Jesse: "My heart is telling me that this is perhaps the last letter of my life. If that is so, I beg one thing from you. When the war is over, please go to Germany, find my son, and tell him about his father. Tell him about the times when war did not separate us—and tell him that things can be different between men in this world. Your brother, Luz."

In 1951, Jesse Owens fulfilled that request. He found Luz Long's son in war-torn Germany and passed on his father's message. Jesse later said that what he valued most by far from the 1936 Olympic experience was his friendship with Luz Long.[48]

Born to Love

Marianne Williamson said, "Love is what we are born with. Fear is what we learn. The spiritual journey is the unlearning of fear and prejudices and the acceptance of love back in our hearts. Love is the essential reality and our purpose on earth. To be consciously aware of it, to experience love in ourselves and others, is the meaning of life."[49]

When you and I were born, we didn't hate anyone. However, I sense hate every time I turn on the news, listen to a neighbor gossip, or watch an elementary-school student bully someone smaller or weaker. Hate is something we learn. That is the bad news.

The good news is better and more compelling: if you can learn hate, you can also *unlearn* hate. The key to unlearning hate is to learn more about others. To truly strive to be empathetic. To try to walk a mile in their shoes. To really connect. Understanding their perspective will allow you to deeply entertain the opinions of others without necessarily agreeing with them.

That's the power you need to make a difference. That's the power that enables you to embrace the love with which you were born with.

Every single day, somewhere on this planet, men, women, and even children are being ostracized, shunned, bullied, terrorized, tortured, and even killed because of their religious beliefs, race, sexual orientation, appearance—just because they are different in some way. That evil tragedy will continue until all of us—like Luz Long—stand up, genuinely reach out a hand, befriend another, and connect.

We have to stop being quiet. We need to defend those who cannot defend themselves.

Let's follow Luz Long's example and promise to show respect for *all* people no matter how different they are. Be a person committed to living with dignity and peace—someone who celebrates diversity and embraces differences among people. Befriend that one person who seems to be a loner—even though she's a bit different from you. You may be surprised; a best friend may be found in the most unlikely places.

I can hear Luz and Jesse screaming from the heavens above: "Hate should never separate us!" We can live with each other's differences—and even develop great love for those who are different. We just need to be kind, civil, and empathetic, recognizing everyone around us as fellow members of the human race.

As was demonstrated by Jesse and Luz, love accepts others precisely the way they are, not the way you want them to be. The lens of love is not blurry or distorted. It allows you to see how beautiful others are in vivid, living color—with both their weaknesses and strengths, their imperfections and virtues. If you are going to love others, you cannot force them to first meet your prerequisites. You must learn to recognize and accept others totally before you will be able to love them.

Likewise, you must trust enough to allow others to love you just the way you are. As Brené Brown wrote, "We cultivate love when we allow our most vulnerable and powerful selves to be deeply seen and known when we honor the spiritual connection that grows from that offering with trust, respect, kindness, and affection."[50]

When love is leading you, your energy toward others is focused on their needs, their happiness, and their well-being, not your own wants. Likewise, if someone is interacting with you in an unconditional, loving manner, that person's loving energy is mirrored back in their direction. This symbiotic loving vitality can grow in strength, power, and depth over time and create a cyclone-like vortex of adoring energy. It leads you to respect and serve each other.

Real love modifies your sense of self-importance; it teaches you that the one you love has just as much value, worth, and potential as you do. When this happens, it becomes just as (if not more) important to you that they laugh, learn, lead, live, and love in this life as you do. Unconditional love is the only force that can cause this awakening. It is the only power that renders hate, envy, jealousy, greed, and egotism powerless.

A Child and a Chair

I learned this valuable lesson about unconditional love early in my years as a father—and I have a constant visual reminder of how I learned that a certain little boy had every bit as much value and worth as I did.

It all started with a chair. Can a chair be part of a family?

Mine is.

His leather is soft, cool, and unbelievably comfortable. Forget the need for Tylenol, Advil PM, ZzzQuil, or Ambien; merely reclining with this guy results in the kind of instant relaxation that promotes the ultimate snooze.

But I'm not going to talk about the heavenly slumber this chair delivers. Instead, I'm going to relate what I'm reminded of when I look at this chair—an incident that causes me heartache, parental pain, and regret.

When I bought the chair in 1999, it was brand-new. The leather was smooth, unmarred, and unsoiled, and I bought a special leather cleaner and conditioner to keep it that way. In the days after I bought the chair, before sitting in it, I always made sure my pants were clean and there was nothing in my back pockets that could scratch or mar the leather. I also cautioned my kids to not roughhouse, eat, or do anything else in the chair that could damage it in any way.

One evening as I was making dinner for my kids, I looked up and saw AJ—who was four at the time—standing in the chair holding on to the headrest and enthusiastically jumping on the seat. From my station in the kitchen, I calmly said, "AJ, stop jumping on Daddy's chair."

Did he stop?

Those of you who have had four-year-old, rambunctious little rascals already know the answer.

He did not stop at all. In fact, he jumped even harder while giving me a mischievous grin that said, *I hear you, but I don't care.* So I turned, put on my most serious face, looked him dead in the eye, and said, "AJ, Daddy said to stop jumping on the chair."

It was my second request. This one, however, was delivered with an ominous increase in energy, if you know what I mean.

Did AJ stop jumping then?

No way.

In fact, he looked at me, giggled, and jumped on that chair like Winnie the Pooh's pal Tigger, with a playful, exuberant enthusiasm. He looked like he was practicing a gymnastics routine, getting ready to vault right over the back of my prized chair.

I am the kind of dad who does not ask three times. If I ask twice and I know my kids have heard and understood me, then I shift gears. Words become action.

So you can guess what happened next. I promptly put down my cooking utensils, wiped off my hands, and strode into the family room with purpose. AJ saw me coming and knew I meant business.

You see, when I get frustrated, I literally bite my tongue. To this day, the kids call out a warning cry to each other: "Watch out, Dad is starting to bite his tongue." It almost always gets them all to sit up, take notice, and stop whatever offensive thing they're doing.

As I came into the family room, AJ knew he was in trouble. He immediately sat very still on the chair. His nonverbal language was unmistakable. He was sorry. He knew that what he was doing was wrong. It would not happen again.

I was about to leave it at that when I saw the fingernail scratches in the leather headrest—the place where AJ had grabbed the chair. That was it. I lost it. I grabbed AJ by his wrist and pulled him to his feet. I pointed at the scratches and virtually hissed, "AJ, did you do this? DID YOU DOOO THIIISSS???"

His little bottom lip began to quiver. I think it was the first and only time he had ever been truly scared of me, but I continued. Holding his wrist firmly, I pointed at the scratches and sternly repeated, "AJ, did you make these scratches in the chair?"

My little boy's head dropped; his eyes were moist. He slowly nodded as the tears began to fall. I said, "AJ, never, ever scratch Daddy's chair again."

With that, I sent him to his room.

I have now had this chair for eighteen years. I have often looked at those scratches and recalled that experience, feelings of melancholy, remorse, and sorrow creeping into my heart. I see those still-visible scratches now and want to cry—not because the leather got scratched but because the scratches remind me of a time when I placed more value in a silly leather chair than I did my own son. They remind me of a time when I placed far too little value on my connection with my little boy.

So what? He made a few scratches in the leather. Who the hell cares? Scratches or no scratches, my chair is still as comfy as ever. Even so, that lesson was more for me than for AJ: There is a time and a place and a way in which to reprimand others. But more than that, material objects are absurdly meaningless when compared to the value of others' tender feelings.

That day, a stupid father scratched his own son's precious little soul with anger and hurtful words. The fear in AJ's little face still haunts me. His tears were bad enough, but what really causes me such anguish is AJ's innocent, tender face looking back at me in terror. My connection with him suffered a tremendous blow that day. Instead of seeing and sensing my love for him, he saw something that must have seemed just the opposite.

I wish so badly I could go back and do things all over again—this time the way they *should* have been done. But, as you know, we only get one chance.

My children are older now. Yet occasionally, with preteens and teenagers in my house, it's tough to remember what behavior is developmentally appropriate. As they do bothersome things, I sometimes feel the frustration building up in me. Then I remember that what they're doing is just normal, learning behavior for kids their age. At those times, I often think of those scratches and say to myself, *Don't lose it just because your kids are kids.*

So next time you see your child metaphorically jumping on your favorite leather chair, please remember what happened to me. Take it from someone who has been there and done that. Do not scream, yell, grab, shame, and scold your child for being a child. Your child will only feel confused, hurt, and demoralized. And you will feel nothing like a loving parent.

In our professional and personal lives, we all too often jump to conclusions. We've all been told to breathe and slowly count to ten. It truly works. When you feel that knee-jerk emotional reaction rear its ugly head, take a breath, count to ten, and then ask some reassuring, tactful, nonthreatening questions. How did this happen? How long has this been happening? Why does this happen? Focus on the problem or issue as opposed to the person. Act with empathy, understanding, and love, and cut the kid—regardless of his age—some slack.

Wise Words at a Wedding

When I think of ways to describe love in all its varieties, I cannot help but think of Paul and his letter to the Corinthians. Consider this summary of Paul's description: Love is patient, love is kind, it does not envy, it does not boast, it is not proud. It does not dishonor others, it is not self-seeking, it is not easily angered, it keeps no record of wrongs. Love does not delight in evil but rejoices in the truth. It always protects, always trusts, always hopes, always perseveres (see 1 Corinthians 13:4–7).

Here's what that means: Your ego is intolerant, while love is patient. Your ego is callous, while love is kind. Your ego is envious, while love has goodwill. Your ego is boastful, while love is humble. Your ego is proud, while love is meek. Your ego is dishonoring, while love is dignifying. Your ego is self-seeking, while love is self-sacrificing. Your ego is easily angered, while love is calm. Your ego keeps records of rights and wrongs, while love forgives and forgets. Your ego is apathetic to honesty, while love delights in truth. Your ego forsakes, while love protects. Your ego is suspicious, while love gives others the benefit of the doubt. Your ego is gloom, while love is hope. Your ego abandons, while love perseveres.

Paul got it. Do you?

I started this discussion by talking about healthy self-love. As I said, healthy self-love is absolutely necessary before you can recognize and welcome unconditional love in your life. The conundrum is how to love yourself without getting sucked into egotism. For me, the key is to stay focused on the definition of unconditional love: wanting the happiness of another with no ulterior motive.

Many years ago, I attended a wedding at which the minister delivered powerful advice to the blissfully ignorant couple standing in front of him: "I want you to make me a promise. I want you to have at least one argument a day."

You could tell by the expression on the faces of the bride and groom that they were a bit puzzled. And they weren't the only ones. As I glanced around the room, the wedding guests were also visibly perplexed. I thought to myself, *Where in the world is the old man of the cloth going with this? Did he get that argument thing right, or was it an unwitting faux pas?*

After making his pronouncement, the minister paused for dramatic effect, as if he wanted the story to take root in the young couple's hearts, minds, and souls. I don't know if they even remember it; they were probably anxious to get on with their honeymoon. But I have not forgotten it.

After a few long and somewhat awkward moments, the minister grinned and said, "Let me explain. Young man, you should always be looking out for the interests, happiness, and well-being of your new bride." Then he turned to the new wife and said, "And you, young lady, should also be striving to place the needs, wants, and joy of your husband above your own wishes and desires.

"So when you have this daily argument, I want you to argue for the happiness of the other. I want you to argue for your spouse's position. If you are choosing a restaurant, make sure you insist on a restaurant your partner truly enjoys. If you are deciding on a movie, again make sure you are arguing to see the movie your partner wants to see as opposed to the movie you want to see."

He went on with some other examples, but his message was clear: love is wanting the happiness of another with no ulterior motives.

Walking the Talk

As I look back over my years as a father, I remember many times when I needed to place the happiness of one of my children ahead of my own—and, as you've seen, a few of those times really stand out in my mind. An especially tender one involved my youngest daughter, Mackey.

Mackey loves all sorts of crafts; she's especially passionate about origami, drawing, and friendship bracelets. A few years ago, while I was relaxing in my recliner after work, she asked if I wanted her to make me a rubber-band friendship bracelet. When I said I would, she eagerly showed me my color options. I chose purple, white, and gold—my high school colors. (Yes, I still bleed Monta Vista purple and gold.)

Mackey sat down beside me right then and there and weaved a simple rubber-band bracelet. When finished, she excitedly said, "Here, Dad—now we're BFFs [best friends forever]."

Admiring her work, I enthusiastically said, "WOW, that is really cool!" I slipped it onto my wrist, and she beamed.

As I was getting ready for bed that evening, I put the bracelet on my dresser along with my cell phone, keys, wallet, and other personal items. The next morning as I got ready, I inadvertently left the bracelet on my dresser. I was preoccupied with many other things and really didn't think at all about the bracelet.

It stayed on my dresser for about a month.

One morning as I was brushing my teeth, out of the corner of my eye I saw Mackey staring at the friendship bracelet, which was still on my dresser. My heart instantly dropped. Did she doubt my commitment to be BFFs? Did she mistrust my enthusiastic reaction when she first handed me the bracelet? Was I walking my talk? By leaving that bracelet on the dresser, had I demonstrated real love? Had I thought first and foremost about her feelings?

I quickly spat out my toothpaste, rinsed my mouth, spun around, and said, "There it is! I have been looking for that!" Yes, I admit it was a little white lie, but it was all I had at the moment. I quickly put it on and asked if it went with my shirt.

When she simply beamed in response, I said, "I will take that as a yes."

"Still BFFs?" I asked. She nodded. I wore her bracelet—along with her smile—the entire day. And I wore it often after that.

The things we say are important, but our actions carry far more weight. Our actions ultimately validate what we say! If our words don't align with our actions, our words soon become nothing more than white noise. Others hear us speaking, but our words themselves become void of all believability. We lose credibility. Connections are severed. Love is threatened.

Just remember, it occasionally happens to me, it happens to you, and it happens to everyone. Every one of us falls short at times. Every one of us occasionally does something that doesn't totally align with what we say. Walking the talk is one of life's most weighty challenges. So don't beat yourself up when you stumble and fall. Don't get discouraged when your words and actions aren't in complete harmony. Just keep trying to do your best.

Another of Mackey's craft projects illustrated an equally important concept. One day she asked if I wanted a "boondoggle" for my key ring. I'll admit that at first I didn't see much use for it, but I knew it was important to her—and that lanyards were another item crafted only for BFFs. So, of course, I said I wanted one.

Spreading out her array of plastic string options, she asked me to pick two colors for my boondoggle. Once again I went with my old high school colors: purple and gold. A week later, she proudly presented me with my own boondoggle—a custom accessory made just for me. She watched with excitement as I attached it to my key ring right away. (I wasn't going to abandon *this* project like I had the bracelet.)

I didn't think much about it until the morning I went to our local fitness center. After my workout, I went to the counter where all the gym rats stash their keys while working up a sweat. There I stood, staring at a sea of keys that all looked remarkably similar. All, that is, except mine. My key ring, festooned with a purple-and-gold boondoggle, stuck out like a sore thumb. I smiled as I grabbed it and headed to my car with gratitude for Mac and her help in making my keys unique.

That in turn got me thinking about my kids. They all share my genetic makeup, which makes them similar in many ways. But they all stand out, just like my boondoggle, because of the things that make them unique—Kelly's acting talents, AJ's athletic abilities, Kai's sensitivity and intelligence, and Mackey's creativity and spunky personality. Their differences are an important part of them and part of the reason I love them so.

Too often we feel tremendous pressure to wear certain clothes, act a certain way, and live by a certain set of rules. We desperately want to fit in, to be accepted—and the inevitable result is a dumbing down of our unique talents, so we won't seem strange or different or out of the norm. I'm so glad my children have talents that make them unique and that they make decisions based on their own feelings without worrying about what others may say or think. And I am equally glad that I have demonstrated to them that my love is *not* based on them being the same as anyone else.

The inimitable Oscar Wilde, himself a unique soul, said, "I won't tell you that the world matters nothing, or the world's voice, or the voice of society. They matter a great deal. They matter far too much. But there are moments when one has to choose between living one's own life, fully, entirely, completely—or dragging out some false, shallow, degrading existence that the world in its hypocrisy demands. You have that moment now. Choose!"[51]

I hope and pray my children will always be that unique set of keys adorned with colorful boondoggles, standing out from the crowd in a sea of normalcy. It's that individuality that makes them so special, because no one else has those exact gifts. They are theirs alone. I also hope and pray they will be deeply loved—not only by me but by others—for those unique gifts.

The Power of Story

I'd like to wrap up my discussion of love with a description of how as a very young child I learned about love in a way that has stayed with me throughout my life. That manifestation of love and the powerful connections it provides came to me in the form of stories. Stories have always been a big part of my life—and one of the most powerful ways I connected with the people I loved.

My earliest memories are of my family members telling stories about their parents and grandparents. My two favorite storytellers were my father and my Uncle Kay; they told countless stories that collectively paint a vivid picture of who my ancestors were. Through those vibrant stories, I connected with my ancestors' real-world hopes, dreams, joys, failures, and sorrows. And in trade, those stories made me appreciate, ponder, laugh, and feel a tremendous sense of love for them.

Sometimes I asked Dad to tell me a story from his youth or from the life of one of my grandparents, but most often the stories came tumbling out in an impromptu way, triggered by a thought or memory that connected my father to an earlier time.

I loved to listen to my father tell stories that made him chuckle for one simple reason: when my father laughed, I laughed. I adored hearing about my great-grandfather's quick wit and what seemed his unerring ability to see the glass half full.

But the stories weren't always laced with laughter. My father also told of the hardships my ancestors faced and how they dealt with those challenges, creating for me a portrait of people who triumphed over odds at a time when life presented unique trials. I learned of their struggle to make ends meet during the Great Depression; I heard how my grandmother doggedly worked twelve-hour days by my grandfather's side in a sweltering, humid dry-cleaning business so they could keep a roof over their heads and put food on the table.

There were also stories of high adventure and antics of an earlier day that captured my imagination. I particularly remember the one about a bull on the family farm trying to gore my great-grandfather. Had it not been for Kate, the faithful old dog, things would have ended very differently.

I treasure even now the collection of stories my father told me over the many years we were together. Through those stories, I learned more about his life than I could have through any other process. I also learned about my mother's life and about the lives of my grandparents and others who form the fabric of my family. Those stories wove a powerful connection between me and the people who came together to create our family, some of whom I would never have known in any other way. And those stories made me feel loved.

Those stories are important for several profound reasons. For one thing, without understanding the histories, hardships, accomplishments, motivations, and joys of those people, it would be easy to dismiss them as nothing more than names on a family tree. But there's another crucial reason their stories are so imperative: unless I understand *their* stories, I can never fully understand my own.

To appreciate their significant influence, it's important to examine the way stories have always been a powerful tool in teaching, leading, and uniting our clans, communities, and even our companies. By emphasizing a group's shared virtues, goals, and commonalities, storytelling knit the earliest people together physically, emotionally, and mentally. Stories united the group, tribe, or community, giving each person a sense of identity and belonging. Stories told around campfires, watering holes, and the kitchen table educated, entertained, and inspired those who heard them, forming deep-rooted and loving connections between all.

Appreciating the power of stories also requires us to understand what a story *really* is. Storytelling is not a simple recounting of mere incidents. Instead, storytelling consists of narratives filled with emotion, passion, and perspective. The most memorable stories stir feelings, seize the imagination, and penetrate the heart with images and sentiments never to be forgotten. At best, stories can be healing and cathartic for both the teller and the listener.

Telling stories to the people we love and serve—our children, grandchildren, employees, clients, and others—is one of the most important things we can do. Stories forge connections. They fuel crucial commonalities. They banish isolation; hearing someone's heartfelt story not only reminds us of our own but helps us feel less alone. We foster inclusiveness by sharing stories that inspire, edify, and enrich.

We need that inclusiveness and connection now more than ever. Our world is experiencing a widening political, racial, social, and religious chasm that fosters negativity, judgment, and shame. That chasm drives feelings of isolation, emptiness, and insecurity. When we create and cultivate stories that drive inclusiveness, belonging, love, and emotional security, we help create a place of safety for the people we love. And that very act helps reverse much of the negativity that plagues society today.

I loved hearing my father's stories—and my kids love hearing mine—because we all crave belonging, civility, and warmth. Stories, especially those told from a personal perspective, bring people together, create understanding and empathy, and unite us as human beings sharing a very human experience. Too often, rules, beliefs, and theories tend to tear us apart, divide us, and isolate us. Stories, on the other hand, unite us and strengthen our connections.

Harness the power of storytelling in your life. Solicit stories from your parents, grandparents, and others. When you show a sincere interest in what they have to share, you will be amazed at what you hear—the images painted, the scripts written, and the warmth and love that emanates from it all.

And the next time you want to connect with your kids, tell them a story. Ditch the theories, philosophies, and rules, and simply share your heart through the colorful retelling of a memorable experience. Your kids want to feel part of something. They want to feel like they belong. They want to be inspired. They want to know they matter. They want you to lead.

And, dare I say, they want to see you get lovingly emotional in the backseat and share a sweet kiss while reliving young love with Nat crooning tenderly in the background.

If I've done my job, you now realize more than ever that true love is in us all. That it leads us to seek the true happiness of others. That unconditional love is the one power that can change us, our families, our communities, and the world.

Imagine a world where all people were truly tolerant of opposing opinions. Where the pigment of your skin was just that—the pigment of your skin, no better or worse than any other skin. Where spiritual beliefs were authentically infused with tolerance, forgiveness, inclusiveness, esteem, and moral civility. Where nations placed the interests and well-being of neighboring nations above their own. Where couples accepted each other unconditionally. Where parents focused not on pursuing their own happiness but rather on serving and adoring those they love.

When you practice the principles of real love, you may be amazed to realize that the key to your happiness is not so much about the love others give you but rather about the love you give them.

I started this discussion on love with a quote, and I think this beautiful musing by Barbara de Angelis wraps things up perfectly: "Love is a force more formidable than any other. It is invisible—it cannot be seen or measured, yet it is powerful enough to transform you in a moment, and offer you more joy than any material possession could."[52]

Remember, *love is wanting the happiness of another with no ulterior motive.*

CHAPTER 5

Living Large: A Delicate Balancing Act

HAVE YOU ever had anyone encourage you to *live large*? What the hell does that even mean?

As I was skiing with a friend a few years ago, he enthusiastically dropped off a ridge studded with signs bearing double-black diamonds. As I slid to a somewhat paranoid stop to ponder my skiing skills and mortality, he whooshed by without pausing. With an uninhibited, foolish grin spread from ear to ear, he dropped out of sight. As I was processing his fearlessness and my impending dichotomous doom, I heard him yell, "Coombs, come on! Let's live large!"

I stood on the side of the ridge watching the swirling gust of snowflakes left in his wake on that crisp, sunny, gorgeous winter day. I thought, *Come on, Art, do it!* And so I did—I continued down the trail until I found a welcome sign with a blue square on it. Living large is not living stupid. I know my limits.

Living Large While You Can

In this chapter, I want to give you the Art Coombs definition of living large. Some call it "living life to the fullest," "living abundantly," or "living a wholehearted life." Whatever you call it is ultimately up to you. I love this thought from the fourteenth Dalai Lama: "Man surprised me most about humanity. Because he sacrifices his health in order to make money. Then he sacrifices money to recuperate his health. And then he is so anxious about the future that he does not enjoy the present; the result being that he does not live in the present or the future; he lives as if he is never going to die, and then dies having never really lived."[53]

I don't care who you are—just like all the rest of us, you have only one life. Statistically, you have about eighty short years, if you are lucky. Understanding your own mortality is critical to living life to the fullest. It was Mark Twain who said, "The fear of death follows from the fear of life. A man who lives fully is prepared to die at any time."[54]

How are you doing? If your number were punched today, would you be ready? Would you look down and be proud of your masterpiece called life? If you were part of a study of elderly folks living in assisted living facilities that asked about regrets, success, failures, and so on, what would your answer be? Could you say you lived large? That you loved your life? That you were content, free, blessed, and happy? That you did all the things you wanted to? That you loved life and grew into the person you wanted to be?

Most elderly people will tell you they worried way too much. They did not laugh enough. They worked too much and did not nurture loving relationships enough. They wished they could have had more balance, perspective, and courage. They wished they had taken more chances on making their dreams a reality. They wish they could have recognized and eliminated from their lives those people, jobs, stresses, and other things that created negativity, sorrow, and loneliness.

So let me ask again: How are you doing? Do you ever feel like you are living in a thick fog? Like you are awake but not awake? Do you wish you had more time, freedom, laughter, adventure, joy, balance, and love?

If your answer to the questions above is a resounding YES, you're not being the best you. You are not living a large, abundant life. Your life experience is yours to create. Why settle? Why worry? Why fret? Why regret?

Before you get down on yourself, let me say this: if you are still trying to figure out how to be the best you possible and how to live a large, abundant, full, wholehearted life, you're far from alone. The sad thing is, we know from literally hundreds of thousands of surveys and interviews of the elderly that most people go through life having never profoundly experienced life and all it has to offer.

It's easy to look at others who appear happy and assume they don't have challenges, problems, or hardships. Here's a secret: people who appear happy are typically exactly that—happy. It doesn't mean they have no problems. People who smile, laugh, and dance down the grocery aisle have had just as much pain and sorrow as people who don't. So you can scowl, worry, fret, act sullen, and play the martyr all you want. That's your choice. But those few who are happy have made the conscious decision to smile through it anyway. Those who are happy choose their happiness.

Everything—and yes, I mean everything—preventing you from living a life you find exciting, full, or abundant is a mental and often physical torment invented, created, and imposed by *you.* No one else. You are the one holding you back. You are the stumbling block. I know that sounds harsh, but you are the captain of your soul. That doesn't mean you can just wish yourself into a new life; it *does* mean you can actively work toward living life large.

As you align your desires, energies, and actions toward becoming the best you possible, you will start to move toward being the person you truly want to be. You will find yourself liking you more. You will find yourself loving you more. You will learn to be more forgiving and tolerant of your own mistakes and care less and less about what other people think.

Steve Jobs said, "Your time is limited, so don't waste it by living someone else's life. Don't be trapped by dogma—which is living with the results of other people's thinking. Don't let the noise of others' opinions drown out your own inner voice. And most important, have the courage to follow your heart and intuition; they somehow already know what you truly want to become. Everything else is secondary."[55]

So stop holding yourself back. Shed the worrying. Live in the present. The past is gone, and you should cherish those warm, happy moments. But, please, I beg you: stop beating yourself up on those decisions that went awry. Make small changes today to bring your life into balance, and live that rich, abundant life you deserve. With small changes, you will find yourself feeling more conscious, more alive, and, more importantly, experiencing life the way it was meant to be lived.

As Eckhart Tolle wrote, "As soon as you honor the present moment, all unhappiness and struggle dissolve, and life begins to flow with joy and ease. When you act out of the present-moment awareness, whatever you do becomes imbued with a sense of quality, care, and love—even the most simple action."[56]

Finding Balance

As I reflect on my life, there are a few particular experiences—carved out from all the other incidents in my decades of living—that stand out as examples of living to work versus working to live. These were experiences where I especially learned what I needed to do to really live—and I think they'll likely remind you of the times in your life when you found similar truths.

During the early eighties in Palo Alto, California, I worked at Hewlett Packard as a computer operator. I slaved away in a cubicle in the basement of HP's research and development lab. Right there in the heart of Silicon Valley, I sat next to the main computer room that housed all the processing systems used by the engineers.

Back then there was an ongoing debate over centralized versus decentralized personal computer power. At the time, practically no one had a PC—and I mean practically no one. To give you some idea of what I mean, one of my colleagues bought one, and it cost him a cool $40,000. Needless to say, mainframes ruled the high-tech world.

So there I was, working at HP—the largest technical company on the planet at the time—as a computer operator in their primary think tank. Right there among the mainframes. Pretty cool, right?

Nah, not really.

Let's get real: I was the grunt who worked the swing shift—3:00 p.m. to 11:00 p.m. My big job was to do system backups on the mainframe computers. It was as simple as rotating the tires on my car or changing the oil every three thousand miles—repetitive and tedious but important.

All those mainframes had to be kept cool, so the floor was raised, allowing another way for the air conditioning to flow into the facility. I can still feel the cool air blowing up my pant legs as I walked down aisles and aisles of state-of-the-art mainframe processors lined up in neat rows. All those massive supercomputers were named after Greek gods and goddesses—Thor, Hercules, Zeus, Apollo, Venus, Hermes, Athena, and so on. In addition to having a name, each had fans to cool it. Each had blinking LED lights that let us know it was crunching away at some new algorithm or program that one of the hundreds of software engineers had fed it.

I can still see the massive bundles of neatly wrapped wires running from each processing god to a sea of cabling under the raised floor. These wires led to the various engineers' workstations, letting them access the CPU number-crunching brains living in the basement.

All those mainframes were pretty amazing in their day, but what I remember most about my time at HP were some of the freakishly fascinating intellectuals I worked with.

There were Len and Sandy—the two primary founders of Cisco—who often came to our basement in the evenings to tinker with a black box they called a router. Once I asked them what the router did. They explained that it allowed two computers to talk to each other. (I should have invested then and there!)

Then there was a guy by the name of Doug, an eccentric individual with an incredible mind and a ferocious work habit. He's the one who bought the $40,000 PC. I will never forget him excitedly telling me that it had a forty-megabyte hard drive—an inconceivably large hard drive at the time. You do the math:

$40,000 for a 40-meg hard drive. That's right: in those days, a hard drive for a personal computer cost almost $1,000 *per* megabyte.

Oh, and let's not forget the nineteen-year-old engineer who had just graduated from MIT adorned with numerous scholastic honors. He was hired to do one simple thing: write critical code that would provide the foundation for HP's computer product line for more than fifteen years. And you guessed it: he did it.

My list of intellectually beguiling cohorts went on and on. I can't possibly describe them all. But I *can* share the most memorable thing about them. You see, during my swing-shift stint, I saw the insane hours many of these folks put in at the office. They came in at about nine in the morning and often stayed long into the night. Sometimes I left before they did. Some openly bragged about working more than eighty hours a week. While I didn't understand much of what they were doing, it was exciting to be watching this zealous, intellectual creativity and brilliance.

It was exciting, that is until my father burst my bubble.

One weekend while visiting my parents, I told my father about some of the world-changing projects the engineers were working on at the labs. That led to my describing some of the people working on these projects—which, of course, led to my description of their work habits. Gloating with admiration, I said, "Dad, I work with geniuses." He could obviously sense I was enamored by these guys.

That's when my father taught me the classic maxim I mentioned earlier: "Art, genius is not being great at any one thing. Genius is being good in all aspects of your life. Genius is being good vocationally, socially, financially, physically, scholastically, emotionally, spiritually, and so on. When you overexcel in any one area, you often create a vacuum or deficiency in another. Being fanatical in any one aspect of your life is extremely dangerous. Many live terribly unfulfilled, unhappy lives while at the top of their chosen profession and passion. We all have twenty-four hours in a day. If you invest eighteen of those hours at the office, you will ascend great vocational heights, but at what price? The true genius avoids extremes and embraces moderation. Fanaticism in anything is unhealthy."

This was from a man who earned a PhD from Stanford University.

Eager to make sure I got his point, my father then started listing professional athletes I knew about. They were some of the most talented baseball, football, and basketball players on the planet. But it seemed their brilliance in the athletic arena had cast a sad shadow over the rest of their lives. One had had several children with various women. Another had made more than $40 million during his fifteen-year career yet filed bankruptcy the year after he retired. Another got arrested for assault and battery, his career cut short by his prison sentence.

I am not trying to pick on professional athletes; many seem to be good, well-adjusted individuals. But my father used athletes to ardently drive his point home in a way I could most readily relate to.

His point? When you are obsessed with success in one aspect of your life, it is extremely difficult to maintain a sense of balance in other areas.

My father's technique worked because what he said resonated with me. I started to look at incredibly accomplished people from a completely different perspective. Those engineers at HP—the ones with degrees from Stanford, MIT, and Caltech—gave Einstein a run for his money when it came to brilliance. But after talking with my dad, I started to notice deficiencies in other aspects of their lives. I saw what it really cost them to work seventy or eighty hours a week. The more I observed, the more I could see that my father was right: obtaining balance in our lives is one of those goals we constantly strive for but never quite obtain.

It's like the circus juggler who rides a unicycle while juggling bowling pins in the air high above his head. While his eyes and hands are dedicated to the heavy pins flipping above his tilted head, his lower half is subtly transferring weight forward and backward or side to side. All the while, his mind is automatically calculating and recalculating how he needs to shift and move if he's going to stay balanced on one wheel.

From where you are, it looks like the juggler is coolly riding a unicycle while throwing pins into the air with one hand and catching them with the other. As he entertains the crowd, it seems he is in utter control and completely comfortable. It all seems effortless.

But when you move closer and really examine the juggler's balancing act, you realize that what you perceived as graceful balance is actually the opposite. In fact, he is constantly shifting, rocking, and adjusting to equalize his *imbalance*.

It's the same for a pilot. A plane is rarely on the exact path needed to go from point A to point B. Instead, the pilot is continually adjusting and readjusting to external turbulent forces that are blowing the plane off course. From afar, it looks as though the pilot has flown a straight line from one city to the next.

But if you look closely, you'll see that the plane is off course, the controls are adjusted, and then the aircraft is once again on course. This off-course, on-course cycle happens many times per flight, just like all those readjustments the juggler needs to make.

You're likely not a juggler or a pilot—but balance is critically important to you regardless of what you do. The maxim my father shared with me is just the beginning. Let's look at a few more maxims regarding a balanced life. Some of them may surprise you. But surprise or not, all of them are crucial for you.

Maxim 1—No one is ever in complete balance.

You may not be tossing bowling pins or flying a plane, but striving for balance requires you to always adjust, learn, move, and evaluate the external and often turbulent forces you can't totally control. All of us have forces that knock us off balance. It's part of life.

So some of the time you're imbalanced. That's when it's tempting to compare yourself to someone else and say, "Wow, I wish I were her. She seems to have it all together."

News flash: *no one* has it all together; we are all striving for balance just like you are. In other words, we are all sometimes imbalanced, just like you are. Be careful, because when you focus your attention on others and start comparing their lives to yours, you take your eye off your own unicycle and pins. And you know what happens then.

Maxim 2—Balance is not easy.

When you are balanced, you are actively processing and adjusting to the external forces around you. You have to recognize the external influences, mentally process those influences, make changes, and take the action needed to counteract those forces.

Balance is action, not inaction. The longer it takes you to recognize, process, change, and to act, the bigger and harder the action needed to pull your life back in balance.

Maxim 3—Balance requires a point of reference.

Just as a pilot needs a true north, you need a true north. You need to have your own core code of ethics that is reliable, consistent, and steadfast. Without your true north, you will be forever looking for unachievable balance.

Maxim 4—Balance is not playing it safe.

Authentic balance is a constant state of imbalance. Imagine the juggler swapping one of his bowling pins for a screaming, grinding chainsaw. Now you're truly *mesmerized* by the juggler because he is at greater risk. His ability to make thousands of minute adjustments is now more critical than ever. Almost anyone can throw a ball in the air and catch it. But throwing four bowling pins and one deadly chainsaw while balancing on a constantly shifting unicycle? Now you're captivated.

Similarly, your ability to attain a balanced life means that you act to regain balance when forces beyond your control push you to and fro. Some of them may even be chainsaws. You know—starting a new job, moving, coping with the death of a loved one, getting married, getting divorced—you get the picture. You cannot simply stand there and play it safe. Life is inherently risky. You need to take chances and be flexible. But you also need to be prepared to have that chainsaw added to the mix.

Maxim 5—Falling is not the end of the world.

In fact, falling is the beginning of growth and improvement. The juggler did not randomly decide one day he was going to jump on a unicycle and throw stuff in the air. He started with a vision of who he was and what he wanted to be. Then, the first time out, he fell. He fell again. In fact, he fell lots and lots of times.

Did falling cause him to abandon his goal? Not even close. In fact, falling made him recognize, process, act, and change. It helped him hone his skills. It helped him become better. So when you fall, you solve nothing by wallowing in pity. Take the opportunity to rediscover balance with new methods and action.

Maxim 6—Balance requires us to say no.

A balanced person will share their time to serve friends, family, colleagues, and others. But a balanced person does not forget about himself. You need to love and serve you as much as anyone else. If you are having a hard time breathing as the plane loses oxygen, you will struggle to help the child next to you. There is a reason the Federal Aviation Administration insists you put your oxygen mask on first before helping those around you. A balanced person knows his or her limits.

Balance is saying yes to others some of the time. Just don't forget to say yes to yourself now and then. And know that it's okay to say, "No, I can't juggle another item without dropping them all."

And nobody wants to drop them all.

Maxim 7—Balance is not vainly impulsive.

True balance is not a quick, emotional reaction. It doesn't involve impetuously jumping to a conclusion.

Balance is calmly assessing, intentionally changing, and deliberately acting. Balance is being levelheaded. Balance is not boasting or applauding success, nor is it ashamed or dejected by failure. Balance embraces failure as an opportunity to grow. And balance means that growth and achievement are softened with unpretentious humility.

Finding balance is a lifelong goal. In math, science, accounting, and any other discipline, we strive for absolute balance. But for me, life is not like my checking account. For me, life is often messy, uncertain, and unpredictable.

Some periods in my life have seemed like an assembly line of unforeseen chaos. And you know what? That is normal. Life is full of ups and downs, rights and lefts, hot and cold, pain and joy, good and bad. That's normal. It's normal for me, and it's normal for you.

In his *Philosophiæ Naturalis Principia Mathematica,* Sir Isaac Newton proved that any two forces are equal in magnitude and opposite in direction. There truly is opposition in all things. Being sick occasionally is normal. Feeling calm and content much of the time is normal. I have low-energy days like everyone else, and you guessed it—that's normal.

While striving to live a healthy, balanced, fulfilled life, it is essential you recognize and accept the natural flow of opposition. It is critical to understand and accept that balance and imbalance are realities for all of us.

Tranquility comes from not attributing too much importance to either state. Simply gauge your imbalance and gently shift and lean toward balance as best you can, acknowledging it as the natural rhythm of life.

Focus on the Present (and Celebrate the Good in Your Past)

Part of what we're all striving for is an equilibrium between the past and the present—with some hope for the future thrown in for good measure.

Achieving this kind of equilibrium isn't always easy. In fact, it's rarely easy. But it's always doable.

Everyone has a painful thing or two loitering in their past. Some have a lot more than one or two. Look at me—in elementary school, I was bullied. It was awful. Not insurmountable, but pretty awful. Thanks to wrestling and the confidence it gave me, I could shift and adjust my mindset and balance. A few may even say I shifted a bit too far the other direction. Nevertheless, there are those who have such horrifically painful episodes in their past that they have trouble remembering anything good.

Regardless of where you fall on the spectrum, you want to achieve some balance—and that usually consists of keeping some things from the past and balancing those with the things going on now. You may need to give some things up—and if you've struggled through the darkest kind of pain, you may want to consider professional help.

But don't automatically assume you need to give up all of your past. Sometimes there are things—even little, seemingly insignificant things—you *shouldn't* give up. They may be memories, or they may be tangible objects. And they may be the things that bring you joy as you strive for balance.

For me, the thing I just can't—and don't want to—give up is the stuffed animal my mother made me when I was a little boy. It is a saber-toothed tiger and was my favorite toy. I carried it everywhere. We were inseparable.

Mom fashioned him after Fred and Wilma's pet on *The Flintstones*—you know, the one who always threw Fred out of the house during the closing credits, leaving Fred to bang frantically on the front door while he yelled, "WIIIIILMAAAAA!"

The official name of the pet on the cartoon was Baby Puss. For some mind-blowing, inexplicable reason, I named *my* stuffed saber-toothed tiger Pickle Puss. (I see your eyes rolling. I hear you snickering.)

That's the backstory, and that brings us to today. I still have Pickle Puss. (No, I am not a hoarder.) Over the years, my mother tried desperately to patch, mend, and repair him as a result of all the cuddling and hugging and endless adventures the two of us had. Despite her Herculean efforts, the fabric is now worn thin. These days, Pickle Puss is now feeble, shabby, and incredibly fragile.

But I simply cannot get rid of him.

I keep him safely tucked in a box of keepsakes on the top shelf in my closet. When on occasion I pull him out, I smile. For just a moment I become a little boy without a care in the world, completely innocent and full of adventure.

My kids think I am absolutely crazy. They cringe in horror every time I tell them his name. Perhaps I *am* nuts. Perhaps I should let the past go.

But maybe I shouldn't. For some reason, Pickle Puss has stood the test of time. He has traversed the country many times. He has moved to and from Europe twice and has lasted through two marriages and four kids. Yet there he sits in my closet, still bringing a smile to my face and a warm memory to my heart.

So I keep him.

I believe the way to live the most positive and balanced life possible is to stay focused on the present—but that doesn't mean we can't make a little room for the good things of our past.

There are times when we need to let the past go and move on. At the same time, there are memories and feelings that are okay to hold on to.

It is okay to be a shy, scared little boy and to need the warmth, safety, and comfort of a dear friend. It's equally okay to be an adult who still smiles at the thought of all those adventures with his stuffed buddy.

I hope that someday when I am old and frail (and have possibly passed on), one of my kids will find Pickle Puss and smile. I hope that when they do, they will think of their father and know that once, a long time ago, their dad was a little boy who wet his pants, was super shy, a bit introverted, and was even bullied. I hope they will remember that their father was once a youngster who had a magical childhood yet still wrestled with self-doubt and low self-esteem. I had my share of positive character traits as well, and it would be easy to list them off. But it is the few undesirable traits I had to work through and overcome that I do not want to sugarcoat, hide, or pretend did not happen.

I want my kids to know that letting go of negative, hurtful, or sad feelings is healthy but also that some childhood memories can bring a smile to your face and a glow to your heart if you simply let the memory in (and maybe tuck it away on a closet shelf).

It *is* possible to hold on to the past without losing sight of the present—even if that past consists of a frail, shabby cat named Pickle Puss. He's my warm, nurturing link to the past.

I'm hoping you'll look for and find your Pickle Puss —the one that will bring a smile to your face every time.

Making the Choice to Live

Balance also requires us to accept that sometimes, no matter how hard we try, there will be parts of our lives that we can't keep dragging along with us. Even when we think those parts are important—like an arm.

Let me explain what I mean with a real-life, unforgettable episode.

I'll just cut to the chase. A guy named Aron Ralston cut off his arm. With a *pocket knife.*

If you think that was a display of unmitigated courage, think again.

Obviously it took courage. But considering the circumstances, there was practically no other option. After all, as Ralston told Ellen DeGeneres on camera, he was facing certain death. And it's amazing what we can do when facing death.

Here's how it went down. Ralston was hiking solo in a remote Southern Utah canyon in April 2003 when his arm got pinned under an eight-hundred-pound boulder. He tried everything he could to free himself. The days dragged by. Hour by hour—127 of them, to be exact—his provisions dwindled. His situation became increasingly more desperate.

On day five, he realized his arm was dead.

On that same day, he realized something else. It was a powerful epiphany. He realized he did not have to die with his arm.

That epiphany made it easy for Ralston to apply a makeshift tourniquet and cut his arm off with a pocket knife. As you can imagine, that was no comfortable task—it entailed sawing through fat and tissue after snapping two bones. But he did it. He then applied first aid and hiked out of the canyon. Just like that.

"It's so amazing to be alive," Ralston told reporter Katie Couric. He'd cut his other hand off to keep the blessings he has in his life today, he says. And here's what he has to share from that experience: "We decide if a [life event] is going to be a tragedy or a triumph."[57]

Whatever that event is, we take it, and we maneuver. We recalculate. Just like the juggler, we shift. We adjust.

I'm confident you haven't had to saw your arm off with nothing more than a pocket knife and a lot of grit. But maybe there are other things you need to figuratively cut off. How many times does something die in your life? It may be a job, a relationship with a loved one, an opportunity, or a cherished dream. If you remain attached to the dead part, you risk dying with it—just as if you, with Aron Ralston, are pinned beneath the boulder.

Aron's choice was to live. To do that, he had to separate himself from the dead limb. Courage? Yes, of course. What he did is not for the faint of heart. But here's the important part: along with his courage was a conscious decision to live—to outlive the part that had died.

After doing all we can to save it, sometimes we need to accept that a part of our life is now dead if we're really going to maintain balance. We then need to cut it off emotionally, apply what first aid we can, and hike out of the canyon.

Whenever something in my life dies, I choose to hike. I hope you will make that same decision. And while you're assessing just what in your life might be dead (or gasping for its last breath), here's something you should never forget as you strive for balance: chances are high that you're doing much, much better than you think you are.

Some Days Are Harder Than Others

It's so easy to examine our lives and find ourselves coming up short. I'm convinced it's human nature. We're much more tolerant of others than we ever are of ourselves, and we are usually our own worst critics. But part of the delicate balance we're trying to achieve in life depends on seeing the best in ourselves.

We won't always have good days, and we can't always operate at peak levels. But we can see each day as a blessing and make the best of it no matter what happens. I remember the day I realized that like it was yesterday.

I rose early to a chirping alarm clock. A familiar thought crossed my mind: *How does the night pass so quickly?* I stretched in an attempt to get my blood flowing only to crash into a blunt reminder that my youngest daughter had crawled into bed with me sometime during the night. *No gym this morning.*

Working out in the mornings is my sacred place. I go to the gym to sweat, think, and sort out the world's most pressing problems. *Oh, well,* I thought. *My daughter is more important than any of that.*

I hit the snooze button a few times but realized I'd never fall back into a deep sleep—so I got out of bed to feed and muck the horses. As I came back inside, my son and daughter were arguing about the breakfast menu. I'd been traveling and hadn't had a chance to buy milk. Once I played referee and sorted out their breakfast commotion, I jumped into the shower.

Emerging from the shower, I realized I hadn't washed my sheets for a week or two. *Disgusting, Art. Come on; you can do better.* I quickly stripped the bed. Toting an armful of white linens as I headed to the laundry room, I walked past my daughter, who was having cake and Dr. Pepper for breakfast. "Really?" I asked. "Is that the best you can do?"

Heavy sigh.

As I came out of the laundry room, my daughter said, "Daddy, I was supposed to make stables out of cardboard for my class's castle project."

Hell, I didn't even *know* there was a castle project, but I said, "Great. No problem. When is it due?"

Her answer? You guessed it. "Today."

Heavy sigh.

"You're kidding me!" I said, not quite so patiently this time. "You need to make a horse stable this morning? How big? How many stables? How elaborate? How long have you known about this?"

Her answer? A week.

Heavy sigh.

By then I was growling. I ran to my room and grabbed an empty shoe box. I started cutting like a madman and lining it with a brown paper bag—you know, to make it look more like a barn. Or whatever. Truth be told, I had no idea what I was doing, but I prayed it would all come together. I quickly fashioned a water trough and scattered some hay across the "floor." I then had my daughter label the stalls with our horses' names and *voilà!* Horse stables were ready to go.

Next I scrambled to make the kids' lunches, clean up the cake that was tracked all over the kitchen counter, and do the dishes that magically appeared in the sink every morning.

Then it was time to run my son Kai to school. After repeatedly urging him to turn off the cartoons and get his shoes on, we jumped in the car. En route, I tried to make small talk—and as was evident from his lack of response, I noticed he was withdrawn. When I asked why, he informed me he had a creative writing paper due *that day*—a paper he had not even started.

Heavy sigh.

"What? We watched TV last night after dinner, and you chose the show we watched," I said, pointing out the obvious. "Why didn't you tell me about this creative writing assignment then?"

His logical twelve-year-old mind fashioned his response: "Because I wanted to watch the show with you, and if I had told you about the paper, you would have made me turn off the show and write the paper."

Heavy sigh. How do you fight *that* line of reasoning?

Well, my much-older-than-twelve-year-old mind ground into gear. "You were watching cartoons this morning," I said. "Why didn't you start writing the paper then instead of lying on the couch watching cartoons?"

I don't even remember his answer.

Heavy sigh.

Next, I tried appealing to his reason: "Son, you will have to use your free time between classes to crank something out. But please, I beg you—let me help you with stuff like this. I'm always happy to help. You just have to give me more lead time."

When I got home, I had just enough time to grab a Monster energy drink for breakfast (don't judge) and take my daughter Mac and her castle stables to school.

As I dropped her and the stables off, I was hit with the overwhelming feeling of being besieged as a single parent. Not only that, but I felt I was falling short in so many ways. *So* many ways. That was my story, and I had lots of evidence to support it.

Just that morning provided plenty of proof. I had not worked out. I had not been shopping, so my kids ate cake for breakfast. I'd thrown castle stables together at the last minute. I had a son who was depressed because he now had to live with the hard consequences of procrastination. To top it all off, I got to the office later than I wanted, and I felt as though I was letting things slip on the vocational end as well.

Oppressive anxiety and disconcerting guilt welled up inside me.

This probably sounds like I am wallowing in self-imposed, pathetic pity. But seriously—show me a devoted single parent who does not feel at times as though he or she is burning the candle at both ends, and I will be stunned into a catatonic state.

Maybe I am overgeneralizing. Maybe there are a handful of single parents out there—people *I've* never met!—who have it all together. They work out, go shopping, do the laundry, make sure the homework is all done, and serve gourmet breakfast banquets to the kids (in clean clothes!) as they leave for school from a clean house. If single parents like that exist, they must be aliens.

There are few things harder than being a single parent. Sometimes I feel so alone in my struggle to balance work, parenting, and the numerous tasks involved in just living life. It is a heavy burden.

What really gets to me, though, is the guilt. I know that some of my decisions (many of which I regret) contributed to our existing family situation, which makes me feel guilty. I also feel guilty about the time I spend away from the house to work. I feel guilty about not being on top of homework as much as I would like to be. I feel guilty for not always having a family dinner during which we sit together around the kitchen table and talk. I worry daily about the effect all of this is having on two impressionable young lives.

Oh, and that's not all. If I start looking back—yup, we can beat ourselves up over the past, too, even when Pickle Puss is sitting on the closet shelf—I can find even more evidence of my abject failure. Even when I *wasn't* a single parent

It's imperative to remember that obstacles, failures, and frustrations are an inherent part of life. If you are going to live large and find balance in the day-to-day labor of life, it is dependent on your ability to endure through even the most frustrating mornings without giving up. If you're going through a rough time, pause, reflect, recognize the imbalance, and consciously shift back into balance. Remember that life isn't always bad. Seemingly lengthy stints of frustration, setbacks, dashed expectations, and distress are really just short-lived, negligible moments of time. They too shall pass.

In times like these, I remember the Japanese Proverb: "Fall seven times, stand up eight."

All Alone for Easter

Here's a prime example. When I was living and working in Europe, I had an experience that affected me so much that now, more than twenty years later, it still hurts.

It was April 1995. I was in Holland, and my former wife and our daughter Kelly were in Florida celebrating Easter with family and friends. For some reason I can't even remember, I felt I needed to stay in Holland. I'm sure it had to do with work—but if you held a gun to my head today and demanded I tell you what those oh-so-important issues were, I wouldn't have a clue.

I will never forget the transatlantic conversation with my Kelly that Easter evening. When I asked about her Easter basket and egg hunt, her excitement gushed over the line. She told me about coloring the eggs. She told me how the Easter Bunny had taken them and hidden them all over the backyard—under shrubs, in the lawn, under the patio furniture, in the branches of the trees. Bubbling with glee, she told me how she and her grandpa had found them all.

I hung up the phone and sat there in our empty home in Holland. The silence was deafening. I was all by myself. There was no Easter dinner. There was no animated conversation, no laughter, no sounds of family at all. There was no Kelly sharing her Easter basket with me.

At that moment, the thought hit me: *Art, you used a pathetic excuse today, and you will NEVER get this moment back. It is gone forever. Your daughter will never again do another Easter egg hunt while she is six years old. It is gone. You blew it big-time. What are you doing? How are you spending your time? If she is so important to you, why are you sitting in Holland in a cold, empty house?*

I was heartbroken. I felt I was suffocating and as if the walls were collapsing in on me. But no matter how bad I felt or how badly I wanted to right the wrong, I could never get that day back—it was gone forever.

I do remember sitting there in the numbing silence, mentally taking note of my feelings and vowing to do better. If she was so important to me—and she is!—I knew I needed to do whatever was necessary to be with her.

You may have found yourself feeling this same way—even if you're not a single parent, and even if whatever you're beating yourself up over has nothing to do with parenting. Or kids. If you've ever felt that you don't quite measure up—and I'm betting you have—take a page from my book.

When my guilt starts paralyzing me, I play therapist. Here's what my inner Freud tells me—and I'm sharing it here because I think your inner Freud would agree:

Art (insert your name here), own your mistakes, learn from them, then move on. Don't let others drag you through the mud or shame you into feeling more guilt. Don't let others make your burden worse with their judgment. You have beat yourself up enough.

Move on, and be the best you can be!

Everyone makes mistakes; guilt is only useful as far as it helps you identify and correct areas where you can improve and evolve and grow into a better human being. Pancakes always have two sides, and so does your story. (Did you hear that? Every story, even yours, has two sides.)

Along the way, someone has wronged you. Art (let's hear it again for your name!), do yourself a favor and forgive them. The burden of anger is too much for you to shoulder. There is no time machine that will let you return to your past and right those wrongs. But you do have today.

Be the best parent you can possibly be today. Go ahead—skip a workout and snuggle your daughter; build those stables out of cardboard; serve cake and Dr. Pepper for breakfast; console a son who feels the pressure of being a seventh-grader and is trying to fit in on top of being frustrated that he didn't do his homework.

Whatever you do, don't let any negative self-talk grip you.

You are doing okay.

No, you're doing *better* than okay. You're doing *great*. Hang in there, and keep doing what you're already doing so magnificently. Recognize the tension, shift, and find balance again.

Horseplay

Once I came to the realization that I was doing a good job despite the times I felt like a failure, I started to recognize ways I could honor myself while simultaneously looking for ways to do better. I wanted to avoid the kind of Easter I'd had in that lonely house in Holland. I'd like to share an example of one of those opportunities because I think it may give you some ideas along the way.

Each of my four children has unique and enchanting interests, personalities, and talents. Before Mac could walk, I could tell she was going to be the animal whisperer of the family. If it's furry and has four legs, Mac knows its language.

Every year, Mac and I haul our horses south to what I call their winter resort. I explain to Mac that we're taking the horses down there because they like it more there in the winter. I tell her that they have furry friends down there and that the weather is so much more agreeable.

Those things are all true.

But let's be honest: the *real* reason I take the horses south in the winter is that I am too much of a pansy-ass to feed and muck the horses on snowy, frigid, dark, winter mornings. So south they go.

The day the horses go south is always a sad day for my Mac. It means we can't go riding for about five months.

One crisp autumn day, I had scheduled the farrier to come and work on the horses. He needed to pull their shoes and trim their hooves before we loaded and hauled them down to horse heaven. With the autumn weather turning brisk and the days getting progressively shorter, there were fewer good days to ride.

That's not all. With Mac in school and my busy work schedule, we were often limited in the fall to riding on weekends. That meant doing some serious time management if we wanted to maximize the gorgeous fall mountain colors as we enjoyed our horses.

One of my favorite concepts about time management is encapsulated in a speech by Dallin H. Oaks titled "Good, Better, Best."[58] Here are the basics: there are plenty of good ways to spend your time—but is there a better way, and maybe even a *best* way to spend your time?

With those words ringing in my mind, I called the farrier and pushed back our appointment to the afternoon. I then surprised Mac by telling her she was not going to go to school that morning. I further surprised her by telling her I was not going to go to work that morning either.

Imagine her delight when I told her that instead we were going to take in one more ride this year. Her ten-year-old face beamed from ear to ear.

We could all agree that school for my daughter and work for me are "good" ways to spend our time. We could even agree that those things may even be a "better" way to spend our time. But for me at that moment, they were not the "best" way to spend our time.

Instead, Mac and I were going on one last daddy-daughter ride before we made the equestrian pilgrimage down south. Mac was ecstatic. Maybe missing a few hours of school played a small role in her excitement, but I promise that her exhilaration was much more about riding her horse with Dad than about missing school for a few hours.

We haltered and loaded the horses in the trailer and let the dogs jump in the back of the truck. Before we pulled out of the driveway, I asked Mac if there was somewhere she wanted to ride one last time that year. After thinking it over for a minute, she decided on Chicken Ranch—a favorite trail of ours that starts at the base of Utah's Mount Timpanogos and gradually climbs higher, overlooking the valley below. It is a scenic route that's easy on the horses and dogs.

After parking at the trailhead, we unloaded, brushed, and saddled our mounts. Mac jumped on her paint, which she affectionately calls Splash, and I swung myself into my big quarter horse's saddle. And up the trail we rode.

The weather was perfect. The fall colors were vibrant. The horses were calm, responsive, ready, and willing. Our two golden retrievers, Buddy and Piper, literally seemed to be smiling—their tongues hanging out, and their tails wagging as they darted off into the brush and scrub oak, rousting birds and other varmints as they tagged along behind us.

One of my favorite aspects of riding horses with Mac is the time we have to talk. For some reason, she verbally opens up on various subjects she often considers taboo any other time. There is an easiness about the time we share together. Maybe it's the mesmerizing motion of the horses as they lumber up the trail. Perhaps it is the tranquility of nature we experience when hearing the creek babble alongside us. Or maybe it's the rustling of the yellow, orange, and red fall leaves lining the path. Whatever it is, we just seem to ease into conversation on topics that would never happen any other time.

We could debate long and hard about my decision to place one last ride with my daughter higher on the priority list than school or work. But I assure you that if you ask Mac in twenty years what she learned in school on the afternoon of October 26, 2016, she would stare at you like a deer in the headlights. She would have learned no math that changed her life, no English rule that helped her get accepted to Harvard, and no science lesson that helped her solve global warming.

Nope—none of that would have happened.

But if you ask her in twenty years what she learned on the morning of October 26, 2016, she will tell you that she learned that her dad wants to spend time with her and that she's a priority. She will tell you she learned how much her dad loves her.

What school lesson could possibly be more important? The lesson that her father will move heaven and earth to make her happy, keep her safe, and be with her is truly the "best" tutorial that could have been taught that day.

Okay, so what about my work? Did the company fall into a black hole because of my absence? Not even close. Closing another deal, editing another presentation, or reviewing financial statements still awaited.

The Legacy You Leave Behind

When I first moved to Holland, a close Dutch friend observed that in much of Europe, people work to live; in the United States, on the other hand, many live to work. There is a big difference. It may seem cliché, but we need to be constantly reminded.

When you are near the end of your time here on earth, you will not grieve losing a deal, failing to perfect a product, or wish you had visited one more client. You *will* sorrow over time not spent with those you love.

Our children do not want the nicer car, a bigger house, or lavish vacations. They want our time.

Words are woefully inadequate to describe the joy I feel when I see a heartfelt, happy smile on my daughter's face as she sits atop her horse. It overwhelms me. My heart wants to burst.

There is no defense in my playbook that is not utterly vulnerable to hearing my kids laugh or seeing them smile. The joy I feel is indescribable.

The contentment in Mac's smile the day of our ride mirrored the contentment in my heart. My life is in utter harmony and balance when my life is filled with my children and their joy. I feel most fulfilled, humble, and balanced when I am physically close to my kids—when I can tickle their backs, amuse them with a silly-dad dance, hear them giggle and laugh, share my quirky sense of humor with them, and watch them smile and love each other.

Remember how important it is to recall joyful moments from the past? These are the moments I like to capture in my mind so I can recall them in the future.

Because I know you likely feel the same way, I want to make you a promise. My father taught it to me, and I will teach it to you: Every unselfish minute we spend with our children, from the time they are newborns through their adulthood, will stay with them for life. These will be the things *they* bring from the past to achieve balance in *their* lives.

An ancient Greek philosopher once said, "Time is the most valuable thing a man can spend." In other words, we need to make absolutely sure we are spending our greatest resource (our time) on our greatest asset (our family).

I utterly blew it with my eldest daughter, Kelly, on that Easter Sunday in 1995. It's not one of the warm memories that brings balance to my life. But it's one of the memories that helps me understand how I can do things better. And while I am by no means perfect, I would like to believe that I am improving at this good/better/best time-management concept. And that's not all: I occasionally remember to tell myself I'm actually doing quite well.

Now it's time for you to see for yourself how well these things work. Take a morning away from your usual routine, unexpectedly pull your child out of school, and go do something your child *loves* to do. Watch your child's smile, and feel the love in your heart swell.

It won't be good.

It won't be better.

Instead, it will be the best way you could possibly spend your time. That's truly living large.

What's Your Greatest Joy?

We started this chapter talking about the delicate balance we call living. Since then it's been a wild ride: a juggler with a chainsaw, a pocket knife amputation, a saber-toothed tiger on the closet shelf, and cake with a Dr. Pepper chaser for breakfast, among other things.

I want to wrap this chapter up by showing you something that spans the generations—something that demonstrates the most important point of all. All those parts of living we've talked about—achieving balance, honoring the past, getting rid of the things that encumber us, and being gentle with ourselves—don't mean a thing if there's no loving in the living.

To see what I mean, ask yourself a simple question: What brings you the greatest joy?

Before I was a father, I would have answered that question in a myriad of ways depending on my mood, the direction the wind was blowing, and the temperature outside. My answer would have changed from year to year, month to month, or even one week to another.

But once I had children, my answer was loud and clear. It still is. It never changes. There's not a millimeter of space for debate, and I can answer in an unambiguous nanosecond.

I get the greatest joy from my kids. My offspring. My brood. My Coombs crew.

My children are my reason for living. They are my air. They are the reason I exist.

I can't imagine life without them.

And somewhere along the way, I was struck with the realization that my father felt the same way about *me*.

I can vividly recall the final few years of my father's life after he suffered a stroke. He was bound to a wheelchair, unable to talk, and barely able to walk. He needed round-the-clock care every day; he was unable to feed, bathe, or clothe himself. In many ways, he had physically reverted to a vulnerable, tender infant who needed continuous care, love, and protection.

While his body was totally impaired, I knew his mind was still very aware. That was the most painful part of my father's last few years. His mind was as alert as ever, but he was trapped in a fragile, weak body that made it impossible for him to communicate. For my father, an eloquent, masterful communicator, this mental imprisonment must have been painful, awkward, and agonizing.

Add to that the fact that he depended completely on others for his physical care. That must have humbled him like no other hardship imaginable.

We eventually worked out a way of communicating, he and I. I teased and joked with him about memories only we had in common, and I knew by the twinkle in his eye and the smile on his face that he was right there with me—when we watched baseball together as he sat in his favorite recliner, still understanding each nuance and strategy of the game. When I commented on something that happened, he moved his head in agreement or disagreement. His body language and facial expressions showed disgust when he thought the umpire made a bad call. On the other hand, he beamed with satisfaction whenever his team won.

I will be forever grateful for my mother's strength and endurance in caring for my father the way she did during those final few years. She was his guardian angel, showing me day in and day out what patient, unconditional love looks like. I clearly remember the times I helped my mother by cradling my father in my arms and lifting him from his recliner to his wheelchair, his wheelchair to the toilet, the toilet to his wheelchair, and finally from his wheelchair to his bed.

Whenever I picked him up and held him in my arms, Dad looked at me with terrified, frightened eyes, as if to question whether I was strong enough to hold him. I could clearly see the words in his eyes: *Art, I am scared. Please don't drop me.*

I had never seen fear and concern like that on my father's face. It made him human, vulnerable, and more of a hero to me than ever. For me, it was the culmination of a relationship that meant everything to me. He and I were coming full circle.

During those times, I gazed into the eyes of my physically meek and timid father, and I verbally assured him that I had him. I told him he was safe—that I would not drop him. I gently laid him on his bed, adjusted his pillows the way he liked them, and then carefully pulled the covers over his frail frame. He always smiled in response.

I often pulled up a chair and sat beside his bed so we could talk. Obviously, I did the talking; he smiled, winked, and nodded. But there was no mistake—we experienced heartfelt communication like never before. I experienced some of the most tender, emotional, and moving conversations with my father during those times.

I remember telling him once that it was *my* turn to take care of *him*. I told him I knew he had comforted me countless times as a child when I was scared, weak, and afraid. Now it was my turn to return the favor and care for him. He looked at me with red-rimmed, tear-filled eyes, grabbed my hand, squeezed it tightly, and smiled as he nodded.

During those sacred times, I told him how much I loved him and how blessed I was to have him as a father. I confided my weaknesses and challenges, and he pulled me close, gripping my hand as the tears rolled down his cheeks. But what ultimately lifted his spirits and generated his greatest joy was when I said, "Dad, despite all my challenges, I have a life that is good. I am happy. I am strong. I am blessed. I am content. I am cheerful. I am free. Dad, I love me. I am the person I want to be."

From his reaction, I knew that this was what he had lived his eighty-five years to hear. This was what he had wanted for me all along. This was what brought him his greatest joy—the knowledge that I had faced down my demons and had emerged on the other side stronger, happier, and more humble than ever. He wanted nothing more than to know that I was truly at peace with who I was.

That's what my father wanted for me, his son, the most important thing in his universe.

Let's move ahead a generation.

If my kids are my greatest joy, and if they are my universe—my most cherished treasure—what do I want most for them? As they grow older, spread their wings, and leave the nest, what do I hope for them? How do I want my children to grow and develop as they become adults?

My hope is that each will someday come to me and say, "I have a life that is good. I am happy. I am strong. I am blessed. I am content. I am cheerful. I am free. I love me. I am the person I want to be."

An Open Letter from an Open Heart

In all of living, in all of loving, how can I help them understand what I want for them?

Maybe an open letter to them will provide some clarity. As you read, watch for all the things that mirror your own feelings. And if you feel so moved, I encourage you to write a letter to your own children, letting them know how you actually feel about them, including the depth of your love and the heights to which you believe they can climb.

***

Kelly, AJ, Kai, and Mac, I want you to be truly happy. I never want you to take life for granted. I want you to have a strong self-image regardless of your education, health, wealth, or career. I want you to follow your heart and listen to your inner voice because it will reveal your true-life path. I want you to have the moral courage to defend those who cannot defend themselves. I want you to be silly and to dance and sing with reckless abandon.

I want you to have mostly positive days and the awareness and emotional stability to deal with the down days that will surely come. When you make painful mistakes, I want you to see the opportunities for self-improvement that follow. I want you to recognize pain and know that you can bear it.

I want you to understand your personal demons. I want you to have the internal fortitude to chase those demons down. I want you to be strong enough to cope with your self-made messes and not allow damaging addictions to enslave you. I want you to live balanced lives. I want you to understand that this is your life's journey and that you are the captain of your own soul. As you choose your destination, I want you to always enjoy the journey. I want you to be humbly confident and treat others with respect and honor.

I want you to love life. I want you to receive and give unconditional love. I want you to love yourself as much as you love others.

I want you to know I will never completely let go. I will always be here for you. I am still holding your hand. I am still here supporting you, loving you, and encouraging you with the loudest voice possible. My hands are strong, and I will never let you down. Just as my father grew frail, weak, and timid, so will I. When that eventually happens, your arms will be strong enough to lift and carry me, and I will look to you for love and nourishment.

But for now, just hold on.

I will not be there for all your trials and battles. I promise life will bring you both highs and lows. I am certain you will feel sadness. The weak and shortsighted father in me would like to fight all your battles for you. I would gladly carry your pain. But if I took the hard times from you, it would rob you of the lessons you need to learn.

I hope you will understand that you must feel sorrow to appreciate joy; ironically, sorrow will bring greater happiness if you fight through it. You will find the courage. You need those hardships in life to forge you into the happy, well-adjusted, strong, content individuals I hope to see you become.

Sometimes I have questions about the universe and what it all means, but I have come to a very simple realization: my father's happiness was deeply rooted in *my* happiness, and he did everything possible to put me in the best position to obtain joy. And so it is with me. My joy—the thing that brings me the greatest happiness and the greatest pain—is you. You are my happiness.

You will face madness in this life, and if you are patient and have faith, you will endure and be victorious. Never give up. Face the dragons with courage and eventually you will win.

Our Creator has given each of you incredible strengths. You have also been blessed with weaknesses; when you overcome them, you will create the best you possible. At that moment, you can look yourself in the mirror and say, "I have a life that is good. I am happy. I am strong. I am blessed. I am content. I am cheerful. I am free. I love me. I am the person I want to be."

***

Those are the words my father yearned to hear from me. They are the words I yearn to hear from my children. They are the words any good parent craves to hear—the words that will make it all worthwhile for you and for me and for all of us.

Someday my children will sit at my bedside and say, "Thanks for never letting go. Now it is *our* turn to carry *you*. It is our turn to tenderly care for you and nourish you. It is our turn to be your rock. Our hands are strong, and we will not let go."

I will be grateful—just as grateful as my father was—to know that I am safe, encircled in their strong arms. But I will be even more grateful to hear those words that so moved my father.

You see, my prayer is that someday when I am old, each of my children will come to me and say, "I have a life that is good. I am happy. I am strong. I am blessed. I am content. I am cheerful. I am free. I love me. I am the person I want to be."

For me, that will be the greatest achievement of a life well lived.

In the End, Human Connection Is What Matters Most

Put it all together, and I have come to know that the main elements of a happy life are relatively simple. They include balance; family; friends; work you enjoy doing; and hobbies and passions, such as exercise, clubs, sports, pets, and religion. Perhaps you love quilting, camping, hiking, woodworking, cooking, gardening, reading, or movies. If so, your version of a happy life would include those things you love.

To deeply enjoy life, we must have connection, balance, and depth. If you love being a grandmother, be the best grandmother who ever walked the earth. It is critical to dive deeply into the activities, people, and hobbies that bring peace and happiness to your soul. We must cultivate and foster these connections so they become the pillars of our full, abundant, wholehearted lives.

I can see you tilting your head, raising your eyebrows, and sighing heavily as you say, "Art, that's easy for *you* to say, but you don't know the challenges and mess I have to deal with every day. It's one thing to say it, but another thing to do it."

Just so you know, I frequently stop, ponder my own path, and contemplate if I am living the best life possible. For example, as a father, I try to give my children massive chunks of my time—but I am willing to bet that if you interview me in that assisted living facility twenty-five years from now, I will most likely tell you I wish I had given them *more* time. When my life draws to a close, I will regret not hunting Easter eggs with Kelly. I would do anything to have one more autumn horseback ride with my adorable Mac. I will wish I played Mario Cart with Kai a few more times. And I will wish I lifted weights with his older brother, AJ, more often. I will wish I had increased my balance and decreased my worry.

Best-selling author and Pulitzer Prize–winning journalist Anna Quindlen wrote about her own parenting and life regrets: "The biggest mistake is the one that most of us make while doing this. I did not live in the moment enough. This is particularly clear now that the moment is gone, captured only in photographs. There is one picture of the three of them sitting in the grass on a quilt in the shadow of the swing set on a summer day, ages six, four, and one. And I wish I could remember what we ate, and what we talked about, and how they sounded, and how they looked when they slept that night. I wish I had not been in such a hurry to get on to the next thing: dinner, bath, book, bed. I wish I had treasured the doing a little bit more and the getting it done a little less."[59]

So let me end this chapter and book by asking the same rhetorical question: How are you doing? Are you laughing, learning, leading, loving, and living large? If not, can you take one action today that will begin to balance the scales in favor of living a genuinely happy and fulfilled life, surrounded by—and connected with—those you love most?

Please do not let life pass you by. Enjoy the small things, because one day you'll recognize they were not small. Take the steps now to make corrective course adjustments so that the remainder of your life is filled with more balance, love, laughter, and joy. Make the decision now to worry less and live more; especially stop worrying about the things you cannot control.

Decide to eliminate from your life those people who bring you down and those hobbies or habits that do not add to your ultimate goal. Decide to fly off that ridge, swish down the mountain, and live large. Do not neglect life while you foolishly chase money. The time to live is now. The time to act is now.

Invest in those relationships that are healthy, uplifting, and loving. Make time for those people and activities that bring warmth, joy, and fulfillment into your life.

And on the way through life, don't forget to look around for those who still need your guidance, attention, and love. Remember the story about my daughter in the bathroom stall?

She wanted to know I was near, even when she couldn't see me. My reassurance gave her comfort that she wasn't alone. Likewise, your intentional involvement in another person's life can provide them with the confidence, love, and knowledge that someone really does care about them. And you get the benefit of creating lasting friendships and positive relationships by paying it forward, all while honoring those who poured so much into your own life. If you listen, you will hear them calling, "I cannot see you. Please do not leave me."

As it is with my children, so it is with you. I hope when you reach the end of your journey, you can smile broadly and say, "I lived a great life. I was happy. I was strong. I was blessed. I am now content, cheerful, and free. I love me. I've been the person I wanted to be." That will be the greatest achievement of a life well lived and your legacy for generations to come.

Notes

[1] In Bob Woodward and Scott Armstrong, *The Brethren: Inside the Supreme Court* (New York: Simon & Schuster, 1979).

[2] In *The Century Illustrated Monthly Magazine,* Vol. 25; ed. Josiah Gilbert Holland (New York: The Century Co., 1894).

[3] In Rodd Wagner and Gale Muller, *Power of 2: How to Make the Most of Your Partnerships at Work and in Life* (New York: Gallup Press, 2009), 95.

[4] *Kitchen Table Wisdom: Stories that Heal* (New York: Penguin, 2006).

[5] In William Beausay, Boys!: *Shaping Ordinary Boys into Extraordinary Men,* (Nashville, TN: Thomas Nelson, 1996).

[6] Judith Viorst, *Alexander and the Terrible, Horrible, No Good, Very Bad Day* (New York: Simon and Schuster, 2012).

[7] *The Mysterious Stranger: And Other Stories* (New York: Harper & Brothers, 1922), 132.

[8] Virginia H. Pearce, *Glimpses into the Life and Heart of Marjorie Pay Hinckley* (Salt Lake City: Deseret Book Company, 1999), 107.

[9] Kenneth Charles Calman, *Medical Education: Past, Present, and Future: Handing on Learning* (New York: Elsevier Health Sciences, 2007), 103.

[10] "Why Laughter Is Good for the Immune System, Opens Inner Cellular Pharmacy," LaughterOnlineUniversity.com.

[11] Cousins, *Head First* (New York: E. P. Dutton, 1989), 143–45.

[12] Ibid.

[13] Aubrey J. Sher, *The Stand-Up Comedy Festival: Send in the Clowns* (USA: Xlibris Corporation, Oct, 28, 2013), 138.

[14] In Brent Q. Hafen and Allyn Bacon, *Mind/body Health: The Effects of Attitudes, Emotions, and Relationships,* (n.p., 1996), 552.

[15] Ibid.

[16] *To Your Health: Gospel Perspectives on Nurturing the Mind, Body, and Spirit* (American Fork, UT: Covenant Communications, 1998), 210.

[17] In John Blaydes, *Survival Skills for the Principalship: A Treasure Chest of Time-Savers* (Thousand Oaks, CA: Corwin Press, 2004), 123.

[18] Peter Senge, http://www.gurteen.com/gurteen/gurteen.nsf/id/learning-is-all-about-connection.

[19] In Chuck Benigno, *Teaching: Excellence or Survival* (Tucson, AZ: Wheatmark, 2006), 51.

[20] Ronald Fagin, Yoram Moses, Joseph Y. Halpern, and Moshe Y. Vardi, *Reasoning About Knowledge* (Cambridge, MA: MIT Press, 2003), 49.

[21] *Connecting Leadership and Learning: Principles for Practice,* ed. John MacBeth and Neil Dempster (New York, NY: Routledge, 2008), 32.

[22] *The Autobiography of Benjamin Franklin* (np: Althouse Publishing, 2015).

[23] Chris Watkins, Eileen Carnell, and Caroline Lodge, *Effective Learning in Classrooms* (Thousand Oaks, CA: SAGE, 2007), 103.

[24] *Man's Search for Meaning* (New York, NY: Simon & Schuster, 1985), 86.

[25] In Charles Bracelen Flood, *Lee: The Last Years* (New York, NY: np, 1998), 136.

[26] Ibid.

[27] In Laura Hillenbrand, *Unbroken: A World War II Story of Survival, Resilience, and Redemption* (New York, NY: Random House, 2010).

[28] In Jemilson Pierrelouis, From *Extreme Poverty to Success* (Dallas, TX: Dog Ear Publishing, 2016), 57.

[29] In Anthony Lopez, *The Legacy Leader* (Mustang, OK: Tate Publishing, 2010), 225.

[30] Jonathan Rand, *Riddell Presents the Gridiron's Greatest Quarterbacks* (Champaign, IL: Sports Publishing, 2004), 18.

[31] Ibid.

[32] Les Parrott, *3 Seconds: The Power of Thinking Twice* (Grand Rapids, MI: Zondervan, 2008).

[33] In Gordon Leidner, *A Commitment to Honor: A Unique Portrait of Abraham Lincoln in His Own Words* (Nashville, TN: Rutledge Hill Press, 2000), 46.

[34] In Pat Healey, *A Woman's Guide to Finding Joy in Your Job* (Charleston, SC: Advantage Media Group, 2008), 44.

[35] Arthur F. Coombs III, *Don't Just Manage—Lead!* (Scrivener Books, 2015), 15.

[36] Center City, MZ: Hazelden Publishing, 2010, 132–35.

[37] In John Mason, *Conquering an Enemy Called Average* (Tulsa, OK: Insight International,1996).

[38] In Bob Blaisdell, *The Wit and Wisdom of Abraham Lincoln: A Book of Quotations* (New York: Dover Publications, 2005), 70.

[39] In Justin Hughes, *The Business of Excellence: Building High-Performance Teams and Organizations,* New York: Bloomsbury, 2016, 167.

[40] In John W. Collis, *The Seven Fatal Management Sins: Understanding and Avoiding Managerial Malpractice,* Boca Raton, Florida: CRC Press, 1998, 149.

[41] Norman Vincent Peale, *You Can If You Think You Can* (New York: Fireside, 1992), 177.

[42] In William L. Sachs and Michael S. Bos, *Fragmented Lives: Finding Faith in an Age of Uncertainty* (New York, NY: Church Publishing, Inc., 2016).

[43] *The Gifts of Imperfection* (Center City, MZ: Hazelden Publishing, 2010).

[44] In Satinder Dhiman, *Holistic Leadership: A New Paradigm for Today's Leaders* (New York, NY: Springer Nature, 2017).

[45] In Laura Taggart, *Making Love Last: Divorce-Proofing Your Young Marriage* (Grand Rapids, MI: Revell, 2017).

[46] *Love and Living* (New York, NY: Houghton Mifflin Harcourt, 2002), 27.

[47] In Daniel M. Rosen, *Dope: A History of Performance Enhancement in Sports from the Nineteenth Century to Today* (Westport, CT: Praeger 2008), 13.

[48] Jeremy Schaap, *Triumph: The Untold Story of Jesse Owens and Hitler's Olympics* (New York, NY: Houghton Mifflin Harcourt, 2015), 235.

[49] Alan Wilson, *Listen to your Children* (Kent, UK: Ascendere Publishing, 2005), 62.

[50] *The Gifts of Imperfection* (Center City, MN: Hazelden Publishing, 2010).

[51] In *The Plays of Oscar Wilde* (Hertfordshire, England: Wordsworth Editions, 2000), 187.

[52] In Karen Moore, *Heartstrings: Love Is Calling* (Nashville, TN: BH Publishing, 2014), 154.

[53] "The Dali Lama: In His Own Words," Biography, July 5, 2017, https://www.biography.com/news/dalai-lama-quotes-birthday.

[54] Stephen A. Di Biase, PhD, A Millennial's Guide to Living the Good Life (Chicago, IL: Premier Insights), 72.

55 Anthony Imbimbo, *Steve Jobs: The Brilliant Mind Behind Apple* (Pleasantville, NY: Gareth Stevens, 2009), 96.

56 *Practicing the Power of Now: Essential Teachings, Meditations, and Exercises from The Power of Now* (Novato, CA: New World Library, 2010), 43.

57 "The Man Behind '127 Hours' Explains Doing the Unthinkable." Online video clip. YouTube, June 21, 2013, https://www.youtube.com/watch?v=mPA07bP-bDE.

58 Dallin H. Oaks, "Good, Better, Best" *Ensign,* Nov. 2007.

59 "Good-Bye, Dr. Spock," Nov. 2000, http://annaquindlen.net/goodbye-dr-spock/.

Note to the Reader

Thank you so much for taking the time to read my book. I hope you've found inspiration within as you take your own leadership journey. If you found the message useful, it would mean a great deal to me if you could leave me a review on Amazon and Goodreads—and, of course, spread the word!

With deepest gratitude,

Art

You can find and follow me at www.ArtCoombs.com

Facebook: Author Arthur F. Coombs

Instagram: @arthurfcoombs

LinkedIn: www.linkedin.com/in/artcoombs

Twitter: @arthurfcoombs

About the Author

Best-selling author, dynamic speaker, and leadership guru Arthur F. Coombs III brings decades of global expertise to readers, audiences, and corporations through his visionary and innovative practices. Founder and CEO of KomBea Corporation, Art has served for more than fifteen years developing and marketing tools that blend human intelligence and automation. Art's best-selling Don't Just Manage—LEAD! has been hailed by some of the nation's top executives, and his new work on the foundations of human connection provides a powerful formula for success that captivates and inspires readers. Before founding KomBea, Art served as EVP of Strategic Initiatives for FirstSource. As CEO and founder of Echopass Corporation, he helped build the world's premier contactcenter hosting environment. Art has served as Sento Corporation's CEO, managing director and vice president of Europe for Sykes Enterprises, and has worked for organizations such as Hewlett-Packard, VLSI Research, and RasterOps. His vast experience with people and organizations has led Art to sharing transformative principles as a charismatic speaker—principles you can now access within these pages.

Printed in Great Britain
by Amazon